NATIVE AMERICANS AND THE SPANISH

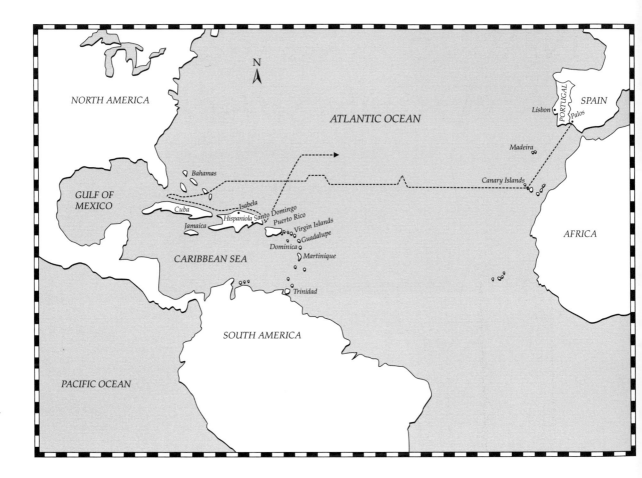

NATIVE AMERICANS AND THE SPANISH

Therese De Angelis

Frank W. Porter III
General Editor

CHELSEA HOUSE PUBLISHERS
Philadelphia

On the cover: This petroglyph in Standing Cow Ruin, Canyon del Muerto, Arizona, depicts the arrival of the Spanish in the Southwest.

Cover photo: Arizona State Museum, University of Arizona, Helga Teiwes, Photographer.

Frontispiece: The route of Columbus's first voyage to the New World.

Chelsea House Publishers
Picture Editor Judy Hasday
Production Manager Pam Loos
Art Director Sara Davis
Managing Editor Jim Gallagher

Indians of North America
Senior Editor John Ziff
Senior Production Editor Lisa Chippendale

Staff for **NATIVE AMERICANS AND THE SPANISH**
Designer Terry Mallon
Picture Research Sandy Jones

First Printing
1 3 5 7 9 8 6 4 2

Library of Congress Cataloging-in Publication Data

De Angelis, Therese.
      Native Americans and the Spanish / Therese De Angelis.
          p. cm. — (Indians of North America)
      Includes bibliographical references and index.
      Summary: An historical account of the clash between Native American and Spanish cultures in the Western Hemisphere including profiles of leaders from both sides.
      ISBN 0-7910-2654-X (hc)
      ISBN 0-7910-4465-3 (pbk)
      1. Indians—History—Juvenile literature. 2. Indians—Government relations—Juvenile literature. 3. Indians, Treatment of—Juvenile literature. 4. Spain—Colonies—America—Administration—Juvenile literature. 5. America—Discovery and exploration—Juvenile literature. [1. Indians—History. 2. Indians—Government relations. 3. Indians, Treatment of. 4. Spain—Colonies—America. 5. America—Discovery and exploration.] I. Title. II. Series: Indians of North America (Chelsea House Publishers)
E58.4.D4 1997   970.01'6—dc21
97-7498   CIP
                                              AC

CONTENTS

INDIANS OF NORTH AMERICA

CHELSEA HOUSE PUBLISHERS

INDIANS OF NORTH AMERICA: CONFLICT AND SURVIVAL

Frank W. Porter III

The Indians survived our open intention of wiping them out, and since the tide turned they have even weathered our good intentions toward them, which can be much more deadly.

John Steinbeck
America and Americans

When Europeans first reached the North American continent, they found hundreds of tribes occupying a vast and rich country. The newcomers quickly recognized the wealth of natural resources. They were not, however, so quick or willing to recognize the spiritual, cultural, and intellectual riches of the people they called Indians.

The Indians of North America examines the problems that develop when people with different cultures come together. For American Indians, the consequences of their interaction with non-Indian people have been both productive and tragic. The Europeans believed they had "discovered" a "New World," but their religious bigotry, cultural bias, and materialistic world view kept them from appreciating and understanding the people who lived in it. All too often they attempted to change the way of life of the indigenous people. The Spanish conquistadors wanted the Indians as a source of labor. The Christian missionaries, many of whom were English, viewed them as potential converts. French traders and trappers used the Indians as a means to obtain pelts. As Francis Parkman, the 19th-century historian, stated, "Spanish civilization crushed the Indian; English civilization scorned and neglected him; French civilization embraced and cherished him."

Nearly 500 years later, many people think of American Indians as curious vestiges of a distant past, waging a futile war to survive in a Space Age society. Even today, our understanding of the history and culture of American Indians is too often derived from unsympathetic, culturally biased, and inaccurate reports. The American Indian, described and portrayed in thousands of movies, television programs, books, articles, and government studies, has either been raised to the status of "noble savage" or disparaged as the "wild Indian" who resisted the westward expansion of the American frontier.

Where in this popular view are the real Indians, the human beings and communities whose ancestors can be traced back to ice-age hunters? Where are the creative and indomitable people whose sophisticated technologies used the natural resources to ensure their survival, whose military skill might even have prevented European settlement of North America if not for devastating epidemics and disruption of the ecology? Where are the men and women who are today diligently struggling to assert their legal rights and express once again the value of their heritage?

The various Indian tribes of North America, like people everywhere, have a history that includes population expansion, adaptation to a range of regional environments, trade across wide networks, internal strife, and warfare. This was the reality. Europeans justified their conquests, however, by creating a mythical image of the New World and its native people. In this myth, the New World was a virgin land, waiting for the Europeans. The arrival of Christopher Columbus ended a timeless primitiveness for the original inhabitants.

Also part of this myth was the debate over the origins of the American Indians. Fantastic and diverse answers were proposed by the early explorers, missionaries, and settlers. Some thought that the Indians were descended from the Ten Lost Tribes of Israel, others that they were descended from inhabitants of the lost continent of Atlantis. One writer suggested that the Indians had reached North America in another Noah's ark.

A later myth, perpetrated by many historians, focused on the relentless persecution during the past five centuries until only a scattering of these "primitive" people remained to be herded onto reservations. This view fails to chronicle the overt and covert ways in which the Indians successfully coped with the intruders.

All of these myths present one-sided interpretations that ignored the complexity of European and American events and policies. All left serious questions unanswered. What were the origins of the American Indians? Where did they come from? How and when did they get to the New World? What was their life—their culture—really like?

In the late 1800s, anthropologists and archaeologists in the Smithsonian Institution's newly created Bureau of American Ethnology in Washington, D.C., began to study scientifically the history and culture of the Indians of North America. They were motivated by an honest belief that the Indians were on the verge of extinction and that along with them would vanish their languages, religious beliefs, technology, myths, and legends. These men and women went out to visit, study, and record data from as many Indian communities as possible before this information was forever lost.

By this time there was a new myth in the American consciousness. American Indians existed as figures in the American past. They had performed a historical mission. They had challenged white settlers who trekked across the continent. Once conquered, however, they were supposed to accept graciously the way of life of their conquerors.

The reality again was different. American Indians resisted both actively and passively. They refused to lose their unique identity, to be assimilated into white society. Many whites viewed the Indians not only as members of a conquered nation but also as "inferior" and "unequal." The rights of the Indians could be expanded, contracted, or modified as the conquerors saw fit. In every generation, white society asked itself what to do with the American Indians. Their answers have resulted in the twists and turns of federal Indian policy.

There were two general approaches. One way was to raise the Indians to a "higher level" by "civilizing" them. Zealous missionaries considered it their Christian duty to elevate the Indian through conversion and scanty education. The other approach was to ignore the Indians until they disappeared under pressure from the ever-expanding white society. The myth of the "vanishing Indian" gave stronger support to the latter option, helping to justify the taking of the Indians' land.

Prior to the end of the 18th century, there was no national policy on Indians simply because the American nation had not yet come into existence. American Indians similarly did not possess a political or social unity with which to confront the various Europeans. They were not homogeneous. Rather, they were loosely formed bands and tribes, speaking nearly 300 languages and thousands of dialects. The collective identity felt by Indians today is a result of their common experiences of defeat and/or mistreatment at the hands of whites.

During the colonial period, the British crown did not have a coordinated policy toward the Indians of North America. Specific tribes (most notably the Iroquois and the Cherokee) became political pawns used by both the crown and the individual colonies. The success of the American Revolution brought no immediate change. When the United States acquired new territory from France and Mexico in the early 19th century, the federal government wanted to open this land to settlement by homesteaders. But the Indian tribes that lived on this land signed treaties with European governments assuring their title to the land. Now the United States assumed legal responsibility for honoring these treaties.

At first, President Thomas Jefferson believed that the Louisiana Purchase contained sufficient land for both the Indians and the white population. Within a generation, though, it became clear that the Indians would not be allowed to remain. In the 1830s the federal government began to coerce the eastern tribes to sign treaties agreeing to relinquish their ancestral land and move west of the Mississippi River. Whenever these negotiations failed, President Andrew Jackson used the military to remove the Indians. The southeastern tribes, promised food and transportation during their removal to the West, were instead forced to walk the "Trail of Tears." More than 4,000 men, women, and children died during this forced march. The "removal policy" was successful in opening the land to homesteaders, but it created enormous hardships for the Indians.

By 1871 most of the tribes in the United States had signed treaties ceding most or all of their ancestral land in exchange for reservations and welfare. The treaty terms were intended to bind both parties for all time. But in the General Allotment Act of 1887, the federal government changed its policy again. Now the goal was to make tribal members into individual landowners and farmers, encouraging their absorption into white society. This policy was advantageous to whites who were eager to acquire Indian land, but it proved disastrous for the Indians. One hundred thirty-eight million acres of reservation land were subdivided into tracts of 160, 80, or as little as 40 acres, and allotted tribe members on an individual basis. Land owned in this way was said to have "trust status" and could not be sold. But the surplus land—all Indian land not allotted to individuals—was opened (for sale) to white settlers. Ultimately, more than 90 million acres of land were taken from the Indians by legal and illegal means.

The resulting loss of land was a catastrophe for the Indians. It was necessary to make it illegal for Indians to sell their land to non-Indians. The Indian Reorganization Act of 1934 officially ended the allotment period. Tribes that voted to accept the provisions of this act were reorganized, and an effort was made to purchase land within preexisting reservations to restore an adequate land base.

Ten years later, in 1944, federal Indian policy again shifted. Now the federal government wanted to get out of the "Indian business." In 1953 an act of Congress named specific tribes whose trust status was to be ended "at the earliest possible time." This new law enabled the United States to end unilaterally, whether the Indians wished it our not, the special status that protected the land in Indian tribal reservations. In the 1950s federal Indian policy was to transfer federal responsibility and jurisdiction to state governments, encourage the physical relocation of Indian peoples from reservations to urban areas, and hasten the termination, or extinction, of tribes.

Between 1954 and 1962 Congress passed specific laws authorizing the termination of more than 100 tribal groups. The stated purpose of the termination policy was to ensure the full and complete integration of Indians into American society. However, there is a less benign way to interpret this legislation. Even as termination was being discussed in Congress, 133 separate bills were introduced to permit the transfer of trust land ownership from Indians to non-Indians.

With the Johnson administration in the 1960s the federal government began to reject termination. In the 1970s yet another Indian policy emerged. Known as "self-determination," it favored keeping the protective role of the federal government while increasing tribal participation in, and control of, important areas of local government. In 1983 President Reagan, in a policy statement on Indian affairs, restated the unique "government is government" relationship of the United States with the Indians. However, federal programs since then have moved toward transferring Indian affairs to individual states, which have long desired to gain control of Indian land and resources.

As long as American Indians retain power, land, and resources that are coveted by the states and the federal government, there will continue to be a "clash of cultures," and the issues will be contested in the courts, Congress, the White House, and even in the international human rights community. To give all Americans a greater comprehension of the issues and conflicts involving American Indians today is a major goal of this series. These issues are not easily understood, nor can these conflicts be readily resolved. The study of North American Indian history and culture is a necessary and important step toward that comprehension. All Americans must learn the history of the relations between the Indians and the federal government, recognize the unique legal status of the Indians, and understand the heritage and cultures of the Indians of North America.

An artist's interpretation of Columbus searching for land on his first voyage.

1

"TIERRA!
TIERRA!"

Late on a clear October night in 1492, with a brisk northeast wind blowing and the moon just past full, Admiral Christopher Columbus spied a flickering light on the ocean's horizon. He and his crew had embarked from the port city of Palos in southern Spain two months earlier on three small ships—the *Niña*, the *Pinta*, and the *Santa María*—on an expedition that no one believed would succeed. No one, that is, except Columbus himself.

Ever since Marco Polo had returned from the Orient 200 years earlier, Europeans had been fascinated with the Venetian traveler's tales of unbelievable splendor. He described a land rich in exotic spices, finely woven fabrics, choice gems, and precious metals, including the most priceless metal of all—gold. The palaces of this fabled land, the explorer had said, were roofed in gold.

The bravest and most adventurous seafarers were determined to retrace Marco Polo's voyages and reach the legendary Indies—the vast region comprising Cathay (China), Cipango (Japan), and India that lay east of Europe. They wanted to gain for themselves and their countries some of the region's legendary wealth—and the fame that would come with recovering it.

The Indies lured Europeans for other reasons as well. It was said that the "Grand Khan," or the emperor of Cathay, had asked Marco Polo to send wise men to "teach him the religion of Christ." Many prospective explorers were devoutly religious and firmly believed that the spiritual benefits of converting thousands of unbaptized souls would be as rich as the material treasures of the region.

Christopher Columbus, a sailor from Genoa, Italy, was among those who sought both material and spiritual wealth. He was also a stubborn man. Columbus planned to sail to the Indies by a route never before attempted:

instead of sailing in a southerly direction along the west coast of Africa, rounding the Cape of Good Hope, and heading northeast across the Indian Ocean—a route others believed was promising—his crew would sail west, across the broad Ocean Sea (as the Atlantic Ocean was then known). Not surprisingly, his grand scheme, which he called the Enterprise of the Indies, met with ridicule and neglect.

Modern legend tells us that 15th-century mariners and astronomers thought Columbus's route impossible because of their belief that the world was flat. Confusion over the earth's shape, however, was not the reason the Italian explorer's plans met with skepticism; the concept of a spherical earth had long been accepted among learned men. Rather, many simply believed that his calculations were wrong, or at best wildly inaccurate.

No one knew exactly how much ocean had to be crossed to reach the Indies, nor how large a landmass lay on the other side of the water. But many thought that Columbus's computations placed the Indies far closer to Europe than was possible.

Columbus twice appealed unsuccessfully to Portugal to sponsor his expedition before approaching Ferdinand and Isabella of Spain. After years of Columbus's coaxing and persuasion, the Spanish monarchs agreed to finance his trip. But they did so only because they believed that their relatively small investment held the potential for enormous returns—the establishment of an overseas trading empire, much like that of Portugal. Like everyone else, the Spanish monarchs were highly doubtful that the expedition would be a success.

Despite the thirst for adventure and discovery that was sweeping medieval Europe, Columbus's voyage was believed so fanciful that few wanted to accompany him. Largely uneducated and illiterate, 15th-century sailors had heard fantastic tales about what lay beyond the known world—sea monsters, boiling seas, and vast whirlpools that could swallow ships whole. Ultimately, Ferdinand and Isabella had to help Columbus recruit men by guaranteeing full pardons to any criminals willing to serve under him.

But after two months at sea, even the admiral himself may have begun to entertain some doubts. The date by which the fleet should have reached Cipango, according to his calculations, had long passed. Although one of the ships' captains, Martín Alonso Pinzón, had thought he saw land on September 25, he was wrong. On October 9, the *Niña* had raised her flag and fired a signal gun to indicate that land had been sighted—but again, it was a false alarm.

The already disgruntled crew was bordering on mutiny; many believed they would never see land again. To ease the tension, Admiral Columbus offered a reward to the one who first sighted land, and now every man was nervously alert.

Columbus also searched for signs of land. A sign appeared on the day Columbus spotted birds. Where birds

uue. Oz vous ay compte ſi comme il auint ſi yrons auant et vous
compterons dautres choſes.

Du plain pain de formoſe et de la valee doubteuſe

A 15th-century French illuminated manuscript portrays Marco Polo arriving in a European harbor town. Inspired by Marco Polo's tales of wealth and splendor, Columbus was attempting to reach the Far East when he discovered the New World.

fly, he reasoned, there must be land, so he altered the fleet's course to follow them. Soon, the *Niña*'s crew members spied a branch with blossoms floating in the water. Then the crew of the *Pinta* found pieces of flotsam that had undoubtedly come from nearby land: a piece of cane, a stick—even a board that appeared to have been shaped by a human hand.

And then, on the night of October 11, the admiral saw a light that glimmered "like a little wax candle rising and falling." He was so unsure of what he was seeing that he hesitated to declare landfall, even though one of his sailors believed he had also seen the flicker. After several hours passed with no sign of land, the exasperated crew dismissed the light as an illusion—or as a figment of the admiral's imagination.

Finally, at two o'clock on the morning of October 12, 1492, the lookout of the *Pinta* cried out, "Tierra! Tierra!" ("Land!

Land!"). The ship's guns were fired. The men scanned the horizon and saw, not far off, a pair of moonlit white cliffs rising up from a sandy shore. They fell to their knees, weeping and praying.

By early morning, Columbus and his crew could see that the land was protected by a coral reef too dangerous to approach. Undeterred, the fleet circled in a westward direction and soon realized that what they had discovered was not Cathay, but a small island. The admiral was not discouraged, however; he believed that they had come upon one of the 7,000 islands that Marco Polo had claimed were situated off the coast of Cathay.

Around noon, the fleet reached a calm bay and the men eagerly prepared to disembark. Each ship lowered a launch to row closer to land and the

Columbus appealed unsuccessfully to Portugal to sponsor his first voyage before finally persuading Spain's King Ferdinand and Queen Isabella to finance the trip. This 19th-century photogravure shows the monarchs and their court listening attentively to Columbus's plans.

Spaniards then waded ashore. They saw before them a sparkling shoreline backed by trees with bright green leaves of a kind they had never seen before. Monkeys and parrots chattered in the branches. Pelicans and other unfamiliar birds roamed the beach.

Columbus and his officers knelt and kissed the ground. Then the admiral planted in the sand the royal flag of Spain and an expedition banner emblazoned with a green cross. He claimed the island on which they stood and all surrounding regions for the rulers and the people of Spain, naming the island San Salvador (Holy Savior).

In their excitement, the sailors failed to notice that they were not alone on the island. While the Europeans came ashore, a curious group of onlookers—

the island's inhabitants—watched from the cover of the forest. The natives, known as the Taino, observed from a distance the strange ceremony in which Columbus claimed the land for Spain. Soon their curiosity compelled them to move closer.

Although the log that Columbus kept of his journey has disappeared, two early biographers—Bartolomé de Las Casas and Columbus's son, Ferdinand—transcribed it, and much of what we know about his voyage comes from them. Las Casas vividly describes the first encounter between Europeans and natives, who came to be called *Indios* (Indians):

> The Indians, of whom there were a large number, gazed dumbstruck at the Christians, looking with wonder at their beards, their clothes, and the whiteness of their skin. They directed their attentions toward the men with the beards, but especially toward the admiral, who they realized was the most important of the group, either from his imposing physical presence or from his scarlet clothing. They touched the men's beards with their fingers and carefully examined the paleness of their hands and faces. Seeing that they were innocent, the admiral and his men did not resist their actions.

Columbus and the Spaniards were equally astonished by the natives. For one thing, the Indians wore no clothes. Instead, they went "quite naked as their mothers bore them," as Columbus wrote. He described the men in particular:

> [They were] very well-built, of very handsome bodies and very fine faces; the hair coarse, almost like the brow of a horse's tail, and short, the hair they wear over the eyebrows, except for a hank behind that they wear long and never cut.

The admiral also noted the astonishing generosity of the Indians:

> They are so artless and so free with all they possess, that no one would believe it without having seen it. Of anything they have, if you ask them for it, they never say no; rather they invite the person to share it, and show as much love as if they were giving their hearts; and whether the thing be of value or of small price, at once they are content with whatever little thing of whatever kind may be given to them.

Before leaving Spain, the ships had been stocked with bells, glass beads, small mirrors, and other baubles. The Europeans planned to trade such trinkets for gold with inhabitants of the Indies, whom they presumed would be unsophisticated and unaware of the value of the objects offered. In the absence of a common language in which to communicate, the Indians' reactions reinforced this notion. Even "bits of broken cask-hoops," Columbus remarked, "they took in exchange for whatever they had, like beasts."

The natives were not only generous, but also "wonderfully timorous" (or timid) and seemed eager to please their visitors. So amicable were they that Columbus ominously remarked in his log that "with 50 armed men these people could be brought under control and made to do whatever one might wish."

But conquest was not yet on the minds of the Spaniards. Though San Salvador was disappointing, Columbus remained certain that they were close to Cathay and its fabled wealth. He was convinced that they would eventually come upon a spectacular discovery—a gold mine, perhaps, or the legendary palace of the Grand Khan. Eager to move on, the admiral and his men returned to their ships, taking six Indians as guides. The next morning, they weighed anchor and sailed on. The Enterprise of the Indies continued.

The fleet's zigzag course from San Salvador—southwest, then west, southeast, east, southwest, and south—took them to a number of small islands, each of which Columbus named after a saint or one of the Spanish monarchs.

One group of "La Española" natives greets their strange visitors with lavish gifts, while others in the background flee in terror. Transcriptions of Columbus's logbook describe the natives as "artless and . . . free with all they possess." Their generosity led Columbus to believe that they could be easily subdued and conquered.

This map, dated 1594, is a remarkable record of the first 100 years of European discovery in the Americas.

The inhabitants of these islands were friendly, naked, and poor, and like the San Salvadoran guides who translated for the Spaniards, they assured Columbus that he would find gold on the next island. The admiral was not discouraged. In fact, because every explorer and cosmographer he had studied had attested to the existence of a great number of islands off the coast of Cathay, he believed he was coming ever closer to his destination.

Meanwhile, the guides persisted in speaking about a large island to the southwest that they called Colba (Cuba). Believing they were referring to Cipango, Columbus steered his fleet toward the island. On October 28, they landed on its northern shore. But all they found there were a scattering of deserted, crudely fashioned huts and "a dog that did not bark." Spurred by their Indian guides, they sailed eastward for another large island.

On December 5, the fleet dropped anchor on the west coast of the new island. Columbus was overwhelmed by its lush splendor and called it La Spañola (the Spanish Isle), because it matched the "grandeur and beauty" of Spain. He extolled the island's many varieties of birds, trees, fruits, herbs, and spices. "La Spañola is marvelous," wrote Columbus:

> [T]he sierras and the mountains and the plains and the champaigns and the lands are so beautiful for planting and sowing, and for livestock of every sort, and for building towns and cities. The harbors of the sea here are such as you could not believe in without seeing them, and so the rivers, many and great, and good streams, the most of which bear gold. . . . There are many spices and great mines of gold and of other metals.

They had finally discovered gold. Columbus knew that if he did not return with it, his mission would be considered a failure. But the inhabitants of Hispaniola, as La Spañola came to be called, seemed to have ample supplies of the precious metal and were surprisingly willing to part with it in exchange for Spanish trinkets. The fleet sailed on, keeping close to the coastline and anchoring at night to meet the natives and invite them aboard.

Columbus continued to be impressed by the dignity and friendliness of the Indians the crew encountered. But because they were far from warlike, he thought them "very cowardly" and wrote once again in his log that they would be remarkably easy to subdue:

> To rule here, one need only get settled and assert authority over the natives, who will carry out whatever they are ordered to do. I, with my crew—barely a handful of men—could conquer all these islands with no resistance whatsoever. The Indians always run away; they have no arms, nor the warring spirit. They are naked and defenseless, hence ready to be given orders and put to work.

Columbus would undertake three more voyages and discover scores of islands in the region—present-day Jamaica, the Bahamas, Puerto Rico, the Virgin Islands, and even the east coast of Central America—but he would never reach the Indies. His fleet was nowhere near Cathay when he first sighted land. Instead, he was thousands of miles away in the Caribbean, off the coast of Florida, near a continent no European knew even existed.

But the encounters between Europeans and Indians in 1492 transformed the world and its inhabitants. For the first time, two enormous continents—North and South America—were opened to exploration and colonization by Europeans in search of wealth, power, and property. Along the way, these explorers encountered legions of peoples and cultures whose existence they could not have imagined. For the Spaniards—and the Native Americans—the world had changed forever.

A romanticized depiction of Columbus's successful return to Spain. Native Americans stand patiently as Columbus greets the queen.

THE FIRST AMERICANS

Columbus returned to Spain a national hero. In April 1493, he led a triumphant procession through the streets of Barcelona to the royal palace, followed by his fellow adventurers and several exotic, dark-skinned Indians wearing plumed headdresses and jewelry of precious metal. In establishing a sea route to Asia (and all believed that he had), Columbus had made Spain equal to Europe's preeminent maritime power, Portugal.

The celebration was short-lived, however. Columbus was assigned almost immediately to a second expedition. Now that Spain had found a trade route to the Indies, the country was determined to establish an overseas empire.

This time, Columbus had no difficulty enlisting crew members. Eager to make their fortunes, hundreds of men offered their services. A few months after he arrived home, the admiral again set sail for the Indies—with a fleet of 17 ships carrying 1,200 men. They were to establish a trading post and a permanent colony on the island of Hispaniola (now Haiti and the Dominican Republic).

The fleet made landfall in November 1493 on an island Columbus named Dominica. The men explored scores of islands in the Bahamas and stopped briefly in Borinquén (Puerto Rico) before proceeding to the island of Hispaniola. There, Columbus had left 44 well-provisioned settlers the year before in a fort called Navidad, built from the timbers of his wrecked flagship, the *Santa María*.

They arrived at Navidad around nightfall on November 27. The crew immediately lit signal torches and fired the ships' guns, but they met with eerie silence. The next morning, they discovered the grisly truth: Navidad was a charred ruin, strewn with the corpses of Spanish settlers.

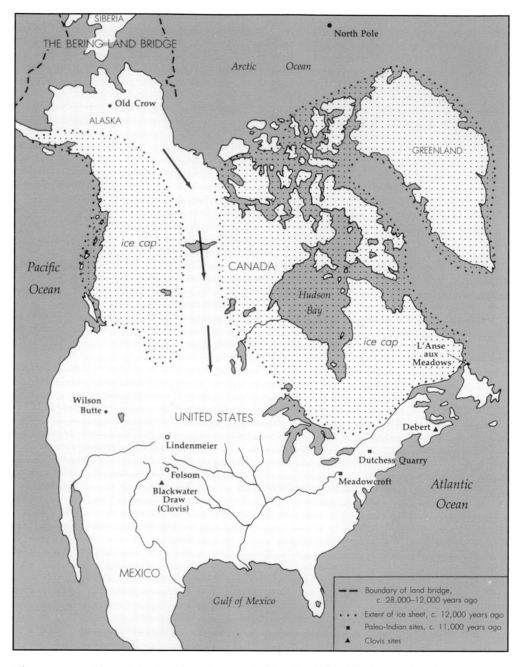

The ancestors of today's Native Americans probably migrated to North America along the route marked by arrows. Archaeological sites such as those at Clovis and Folsom have yielded discoveries that reinforce this theory.

Columbus pieced together the grim history. Eager to find a fortune in gold, unwilling to plant or hunt, the settlers, it appeared, had repeatedly raided the countryside, pressing the Indians into service as slaves and stealing their women and gold. The disgusted natives responded by ambushing the raiders and slaying the remaining occupants of the fort.

Virtually from his first encounter with the people of the New World, Columbus had noted their gentle and trusting nature—and consequently, how easily they could be conquered. After the incident at Navidad, the Spanish were forced to realize that the character of the Indians was of a complexity equal to their own.

The Indians known to Columbus and his peers represented only a fraction of the varied peoples and cultures of the Americas. Some of these cultures had developed long before Columbus's arrival in the New World. Recent archaeological evidence suggests that their ancestors began migrating from northeastern Asia between 20,000 and 12,000 years ago on a voyage that took them across what are now the Bering and Chukchi Seas to North America. These Paleo-Indians (of the Stone Age or Paleolithic era) probably had no idea that they had reached a new continent. More likely, they simply moved to North America over many generations as they searched for food, following the migratory patterns of waterfowl and the movements of game herds like caribou, bison, wild horses, tapirs, giant sloths, and mastodons (prehistoric elephant-like mammals).

The Paleo-Indians eventually made their way down the length of the continent, across what is now Central America, and into South America. With plentiful food sources and vast stretches of land available, they could expand almost without hindrance.

Two accidental discoveries in the early 20th century reinforce the theory that the first North Americans arrived during the late Paleolithic period. In 1927, archaeologists near Folsom, New Mexico, discovered what appeared to be arrowheads, together with the bones of a type of bison that became extinct 10,000 years ago. The arrowheads turned out to be spear points made of chipped stone called chert, or flint. Their discovery proved that human hunters existed in North America around 10,000 years ago.

In 1932, a similar discovery was made near Clovis, New Mexico: handmade stone weapons, including projectile points, together with the bones of extinct mammoths, camels, and other animals. The Clovis discoveries were believed to be about 12,000 years old, slightly older than those of Folsom. The North American inhabitants of this era were named the Clovis people after this discovery.

Folsom and Clovis points have since been found throughout North America; some have even been uncovered in the Andes Mountains and Tierra del Fuego in South America.

Another important tool of the Clovis people was the atlatl, or spear thrower, a short shaft of wood with a hook at one end. The hunter would rest the butt of the spear on the hook and use the atlatl to throw the spear, allowing the thrower to launch the spear faster and farther than he could with his own arm. The bow and arrow, commonly associated with Native Americans, did not appear until around 5500 B.C.

The animals killed by early nomads provided more than food. The hide of a large mammal was made into garments and shelters and its bones into tools, weapons, and ornaments. Along with projectile points and spears, the Clovis people used an array of other tools, such as hammers, anvils, drills, awls, variously shaped knives, and needles made of bone. They employed scrapers to clean hides; gravers to pierce hides and to plane and cut slots in bone or antlers; and spokeshaves, for shaping smooth wooden shafts into spears and lances. They left pictographs (drawings on stone), petroglyphs (carvings in stone), trails, and graves as well.

From such archaeological evidence, historians conclude that the Paleo-Indians were light travelers who depended on a variety of portable and carefully crafted tools for survival. As some of these hunters moved eastward and found more stable populations of small game animals, they began living in relatively permanent homes.

Though many scientists believe that most of the Indians of North and South America are descended from the Paleo-

Indians, later waves of immigrants may be ancestors of some of today's Native Americans. The Athapaskans, who arrived around 10,000 years ago, are believed to be the forebears of today's Northwest Coast and Athapaskan Indian peoples; the Eskimo-Aleut, who arrived around the same time or later, are ancestors of the Aleut and the Inuit (formerly called Eskimo).

By 6000 or 5000 B.C., many of the great mammoths of North America had become extinct. To animals that had not evolved near developing human hunters, the Paleo-Indians were new and dangerous predators. The animals probably lacked adequate defenses against the hunters with their stone-tipped spears. Moreover, the animals were unable to adapt quickly enough to the earth's increasingly warm climate.

Meanwhile, marine life became more abundant. The Paleo-Indians developed hide or bark canoes for hunting and fishing on lakes, rivers, and coastal seas. They began eating a wider variety of foods, including nuts, berries, seeds, fruits, and grasses, and they harvested wild plants each season.

Historians call the period from 5000 to 1000 B.C. the Archaic period. During this time, the inhabitants of North America began diverging into distinct groups with separate cultures. The Cochise people of what is now Arizona and New Mexico are probably the ancestors of today's Southwest Indians. They were expert gatherers and knew how to grind seeds and nuts into flour. They practiced the arts of weaving and

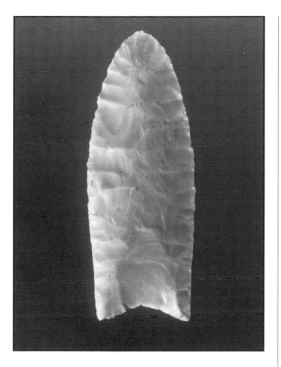

A Clovis projectile point.

pottery making. And the Cochise may have been the first North American farmers: there is evidence that they learned how to cultivate corn.

Another group, known as the Eastern Woodland culture, occupied present-day southeastern Canada and New England, sometimes stretching as far south as Alabama and Florida. They adapted to life in many different environments and climates, using a wide variety of plants and animals and modifying many types of stone tools to specific purposes.

The Formative period, from 1000 B.C. to A.D 1000, marked a dramatic change in human society. With the development of agriculture, North Americans no longer needed to wander in search of food. Instead, large groups of people began settling in permanent communities, where they developed complex social arrangements. During this period, religion, arts, and crafts flourished, and communities began trading products and goods with one another, exposing themselves to other customs, ideas, and technologies.

With increasingly organized religions and rituals came perhaps the most striking development of the Formative period: the building of huge burial mounds out of earth, stones, or shells. The presence of burial mounds indicates a structured society with an organized labor force. The practice of constructing them was not confined to one region or community; it appears to have been prevalent throughout North America. The earliest and most plainly constructed mounds were tombs, but later, more elaborate ones that had flat tops or were shaped to represent animals or symbols probably served as temple sites.

We know of several cultures that flourished during this period. From about 1000 B.C. to A.D. 200, the Adena people of the Ohio River valley built some of the largest known burial mounds. The Hopewell people, who occupied the Midwest from the Great Lakes to the Gulf of Mexico between 500 and 200 B.C., are known for their fine wood, bone, and metal craftsmanship; their complex society featured a class system, craft guilds, and trade centers where people from far and wide gathered to barter.

The Mississippian culture, which arose around A.D. 600, is named for its beginnings in the Mississippi valley. From there it spread through present-day Oklahoma, Illinois, Wisconsin, Ohio, Tennessee, and North Carolina. One of its centers, in Cahokia, Illinois, features a mound 1,000 feet long and 700 feet wide, rising 100 feet into the air. As many as 40,000 people may have lived here in the 13th century, making it the largest settlement in North America.

The Mississippians and certain other cultures, such as the Hohokam,

Petroglyphs on a sandstone outcropping in Wyoming provide a glimpse into the life of ancient Indians.

Mogollon, and Anasazi cultures of the West and Southwest, were able to flourish because they lived in fertile areas that supplied large food bases. Others, such as the inhabitants of present-day Nevada and Utah, were fortunate merely to survive in the harsh environments of their territories.

Similar cultures also formed in Mexico, Central America, and South America. Like northern groups, most of these peoples hunted, farmed, and lived in small communities connected by trade. But a handful of larger, better-

The Great Serpent Mound uncoils in a woodland near Cincinnati, Ohio. The 1,000-year-old Adena mound is a quarter-mile long, 30 feet wide, and 5 feet high.

organized, and more sophisticated cultures grew into empires and eventually gained control of these regions: the Aztec, who replaced the Olmec and Toltec civilizations in central Mexico and established a splendid capital in the center of a lake in present-day Mexico City; the Maya, whose highly advanced civilization produced skilled astronomers and mathematicians, great stone pyramids, and a complex mythology and religion; and the Inca of South America, a vast empire stretching from present-day Colombia to Bolivia and connected by a system of highways.

While these remarkable civilizations were developing, the northern cultures of the Formative period were dissolving, their peoples diverging into scores of tribal groups, which in turn split into the many hundreds of Native American tribes we know today.

By about A.D. 1000, the inhabitants of North America had formed what are called culture areas: regions in which people share cultural traits of a common background or environment. Members of culture areas usually share languages and religious beliefs and organize into similar economic, social, and political groups.

Anthropologists divide North America into 10 culture areas from which modern American Indian societies have developed: Artic, Subarctic, Northwest Coast, California, Plateau, Great Basin, Southwest, Plains, Southeast, and Northeast–Great Lakes. Another culture area called Mesoamerica covers parts of present-day Mexico and Central America, where Columbus first made landfall.

The Spanish incursion that began with Columbus's discovery launched later waves of exploration that affected nearly all of these culture areas. North America would be irrevocably changed by the arrival of the Europeans.

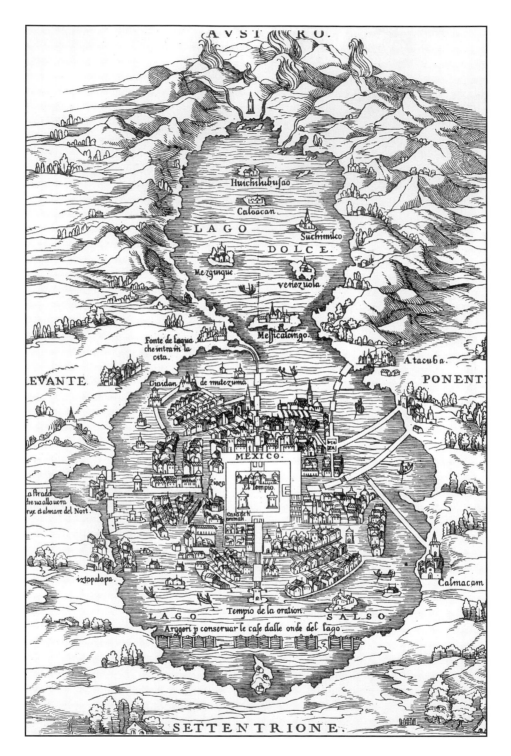

An early map of Mexico City, which the Spanish built on the site of the Aztec capital of Tenochtitlán. The island city, a marvel of pre-Columbian engineering, was linked to the mainland by causeways. The Aztecs also built the dike depicted near the bottom of the map to control flooding.

THE CURE
OF GOLD

Despite the disaster at Navidad, Columbus's assessment of the Indians as gentle and trusting was accurate in many respects. The Arawak were a peaceful society, occupying many of the islands in the West Indies—the chain of islands stretching from the southern tip of Florida to the northern tip of South America. They had relatives (members of the same culture area) in Central and South America. The Arawak living on the islands called themselves the Taino (from their own word for "good" or "noble"). They took up arms only when necessary.

Living in small villages of 10 to 15 families, the Arawak were overseen by village officials known as *caciques*. They had a remarkably efficient and productive agricultural system, growing root crops such as manioc, potatoes, and sweet potatoes to prevent erosion and replenish the soil with nutrients, and leafy crops such as beans, corn, and tobacco to provide shade from the powerful Caribbean sunlight. Their diet also included a wide variety of fish, shellfish, mammals, and waterfowl. The Arawak were skilled and ingenious fishermen and hunters. To catch large sea turtles, for example, they trained remoras, small fish with sticky patches on their heads, to swim under turtles and attach themselves to them. Using a line attached to the remoras, the Arawak then pulled the giant turtles to the surface.

The Arawak lived in homes made of palm trees and cane plants and slept in hammocks made of twisted cotton. In the warm climate, they required very little clothing; men and children usually went naked, while women wore aprons made of grass, leaves, or cotton. Both men and women wore jewelry made of shells, bones, stone, clay, or braided cotton. Chiefs wore ornaments of hammered gold or copper.

Because they lived harmoniously and were extremely proficient farmers and hunters, the Arawak flourished: modern estimates place their number between three million and eight million by the time the Spaniards arrived. The Arawak willingly shared their knowledge and possessions, and the Spaniards learned a great deal from them. They had never before seen or heard of corn,

An 18th-century engraving of the Timucua Indians of present-day Florida during a spring planting. Like the Arawak, the Timucua were hunter-gatherers and farmers.

potatoes, or tobacco, and they adapted the comfortable Arawak hammock for use on their ships.

The Spaniards did not return the kindnesses bestowed on them by the Arawak people. Columbus had great difficulty getting his men to perform the manual labor necessary for establishing a new coastal city on Hispaniola. According to Ferdinand, Columbus's son and biographer, the would-be colonists "had embarked on the voyage with the idea that as soon as they landed they could load themselves with gold and return home rich" and were thus "disgruntled at having to work on the construction of the new town." Chores like clearing and planting land or raising buildings were considered peasant tasks—inappropriate for them but perfectly suited to the Indians.

The Spaniards forced Arawak men and women to provide labor and services in their own land and then compounded their crimes by enslaving natives and selling them to buyers in Spain. In February 1495, for example, Columbus and his men rounded up 1,600 Arawak for a shipment to Europe. But according to Michele de Cuneo, a member of Columbus's crew, the ships could not hold this number, so only 550 of "the best males and females" were led in chains aboard the vessels. As for the rest, it was announced that whoever wanted them could take them. Cuneo recounts the horrified reactions of the remaining Arawak:

> [W]hen everyone had been supplied there [were] some 400 [Indians] left to whom permission was granted to go wherever they wanted. Among them were many women who had infants at their breast. They, in order the better to escape us, since they were afraid we would turn to catch them again, left their infants anywhere on the ground and started to flee like desperate people.

Eventually, the Spanish monarchs opposed enslavement and enacted a new system, called the *encomienda*, under which Indians were commended, or given, to the colonists by royal command. In theory, this would establish a system of "mutual" responsibility in which the Indians would work in mines or on farms in exchange for basic provisions and instruction in Christianity. In practice, however, the new system differed little from slavery; under both forms of involuntary servitude, Indians died in great numbers from hunger and overwork.

Death in battle also reduced their numbers. The Arawak could not prevail against the superior weaponry and experience of the white men. The Spanish built fortifications throughout the island. From these fortresses they hunted down native rebels and runaway slaves who attempted to hide in the hills on the fertile northeast end of the island, a province known as Higüey. By 1500, the Spanish *conquistadores* (conquerors) had established at least seven such fortresses on Hispaniola. They hung rebellious Arawak from gallows, "just high enough for their feet to nearly touch the ground." While the Indians slowly suffocated, the Spaniards piled kindling beneath their feet and set it on fire, burning them alive.

The Spanish carried into the New World something even more deadly than weapons: germs. The infectious agents that cause diseases such as influenza, measles, typhoid, pneumonia, tuberculosis, diphtheria, and especially smallpox were foreign to these regions. Thus the populations living there had developed no immunity to them the way the Europeans had. By their mere presence, the Spanish (and subsequent European explorers) were unwitting vehicles of "germ warfare." European-borne diseases, especially smallpox, swept through the native populations. By 1514, only two decades after Columbus first arrived, the Arawak population of Hispaniola had dropped from millions to 28,000; in Borinquén, it had dropped from an estimated 300,000 to 4,000.

Forty years later, the Arawak were gone, decimated by disease, murder, hunger, and slavery. Hispaniola was populated solely by the Spanish, their European competitors (the French), and, not long after, the hundreds of thousands of black Africans the Europeans would import as slaves to replace the eradicated Indian labor force.

Native American healers employ traditional methods such as steaming, sucking out poisons, and inhaling medicinal herbs in an attempt to cure their patients. Because they had no immunities to infectious agents like smallpox, influenza, and measles, the native population in the New World was decimated by these and other European-borne diseases.

Ponce de León and some of his crew members are shown here drinking goblets of water from the fabled Fountain of Youth. Although Ponce de León discovered neither eternal youth nor gold, he was the first European to arrive on the Florida peninsula.

Among the many volunteers for Columbus's second voyage was a young gentleman named Juan Ponce de León. As a young man, Ponce de León was a soldier of the *Reconquista*, the military crusade to drive the Moors from the Iberian Peninsula, and in 1492, he took part in the Catholic overthrow of Granada, the last stronghold of Islam in Spain. In Hispaniola, Ponce de León led the campaign against the Arawak of the Higuëy province, for which he was awarded a lieutenancy.

In 1506 or 1508, Ponce de León sailed for Borinquén, where he had heard there were vast stores of gold. With the help of the local caciques, who had surrendered to the Europeans, he subjugated the native population within a year. For his efforts, King Ferdinand appointed Ponce de León governor of the newly named Puerto Rico.

It was on this island that Ponce de León first heard about the "Fountain of Youth," supposedly on a nearby island called Bimini, whose waters restored vigor to aging men. (Though the tale may seem outlandish by today's standards, myths about restorative waters and other fantastic wonders were prevalent in nearly every 16th-century culture.) Ponce de León sailed for Bimini on March 3, 1513.

After a month's travel, the fleet anchored off a previously uncharted coast and took possession of the land for Spain. Because it was the Catholic feast day of Pascua Florida (the Easter of Flowers), Ponce de León named the land Florida. In addition to his quest for gold and the Fountain of Youth, he hoped to establish a colony. But Ponce de León returned to Puerto Rico, having discovered neither gold nor the Fountain of Youth and failing in his effort to found a colony. He had, however, encountered at least two Indian tribes: the Calusa, a mysterious tribe believed to practice cannibalism; and the Timucua, a confederacy of as many as 150 different villages that shared a common language. In one of many skirmishes between the uninvited newcomers and the Calusa, the conquistador sustained an arrow wound in the thigh. He died in July 1521 in Havana, Cuba, where he had gone to recover.

Other ambitious explorers visited Florida around the time of Ponce de León's journeys. One such expedition sailed from Cuba in 1517 under the command of Hernández de Córdoba. Accounts vary as to the purpose of Córdoba's voyage. Some historians believe he sailed in search of Indian slaves, while others say he sought gold, pearls, and new lands. In either case, Córdoba's party met with an unfriendly welcome upon reaching the coast. When the well-armed Spaniards landed on the Yucatán Peninsula (southeastern Mexico extending into Belize and Guatemala), Mayan Indians ambushed them. Only half of the crew survived, and most of them were badly wounded.

The fleet sailed across the Gulf of Mexico to safety in a southwest Florida bay but was attacked by the Calusa, who were angry over previous raids by Ponce de León. The Spanish were overrun and retreated to their ships; nearly all of them, including Córdoba, later died of their wounds.

The expedition's untimely end did not blunt the importance of the voyage, however. The survivors brought back gold and idols and fabulous tales of skilled Indian craftsmen and large towns built entirely of stone. As incredible as the stories seemed, the stolen artifacts offered proof of the riches that awaited the Spaniards in the Yucatán. After almost 30 years of exploration, it seemed that someone had discovered the land of gold at last.

Among those who saw an unparalleled chance for wealth and glory was Hernán Cortés, who would earn a reputation as one of the most resourceful and ruthless of the conquistadores. Cortés's thirst for wealth and glory was legendary. "We Spanish suffer from a disease of the heart which can be cured only by gold," he once declared. Cortés's encounter with the powerful Aztecs of Mexico would mark one of the

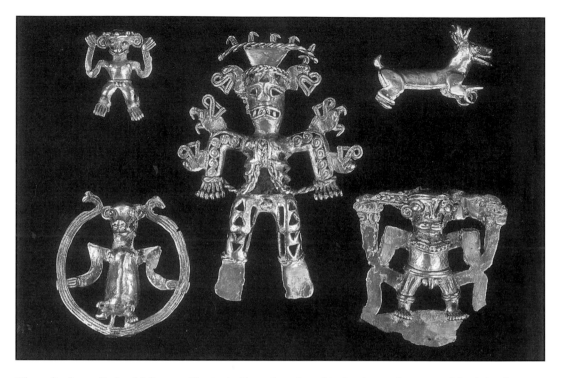

These finely crafted gold figures illustrate the cultural sophistication and vast wealth of the Aztec Empire. The lure of riches such as these was the primary force behind Cortés's campaign. "We Spanish suffer from a disease of the heart which can be cured only by gold," he declared.

bloodiest chapters in Spanish and Native American history—and would destroy one of the most sophisticated civilizations ever known.

Hernán Cortés was a favored secretary to Lieutenant Diego Velásquez, one of the earliest—and wealthiest—settlers in the Indies. In 1511, Velásquez took possession of Cuba (then called Fernandina), an island of rich soil with a friendly and peaceful Indian population that was easily subdued. Through his affiliation with Velásquez, Cortés himself soon became one of the wealthiest and most prominent citizens in Cuba.

In 1517, when word of Córdoba's expedition reached the island, Velásquez assigned Cortés to gain control of the Yucatán. In Cortés, Velásquez had found a natural leader, a man who was as shrewd as he was determined. Over the years, Cortés had acquired invaluable knowledge and experience and had built a solid trust between himself and the soldiers he would soon command.

Velásquez had ordered Cortés only to search the Yucatán for the members of the previous expedition, claim the land for Spain, and convert the natives—no more. He was not to mistreat the

Indians, take their women, or steal their gold. But Cortés had other ideas. Before embarking on the expedition, he revealed his intentions in an address to his men. "If you do not abandon me, I shall not abandon you," he said. "I shall make you in a very short time the richest of all men who have crossed the seas, and of all the armies that have here made war."

In 1519, Cortés, with 600 men and 16 horses in 11 ships, arrived on the Yucatán. The Spaniards mowed down the first natives they encountered—Mayan Indians—with muskets and cannons, until the ground was covered with corpses. Having never seen horses, the remaining natives believed each man astride a horse to be a single, horrible monster. They panicked, throwing down their weapons and fleeing into the forest.

A fortunate encounter that would later prove crucial to Cortés's success occurred after an early skirmish with the Mayans. Jerónimo de Aguilar, the sole survivor of a shipwreck eight years before, emerged from the jungle and joined his countrymen. Having lived among the Mayans for so long, he spoke their language, and Cortés now had a translator. Later, the Mayans would present the conquistador with a young woman named Malintzín, whom the Spanish called Doña Marina. An Aztec, she had been sold to the Mayans years before. She thus spoke both Mayan and Nahuatl, the Aztec tongue. With Aguilar and Doña Marina translating, Cortés would be able to communicate with the Aztecs.

Cortés had no difficulty converting the first terrified Indians he fought to Christianity. That done, he distributed the women like trinkets among the Spanish warriors, then collected all of their gold, which they freely gave. But the gold was not enough. The fleet sailed west from the Yucatán, and in April 1519 it arrived in a harbor that Cortés named Veracruz ("True Cross"). He was greeted by representatives of the Aztec Empire, who wore richly decorated robes and golden ornaments. They told him of their capital 200 miles inland. Cortés set out to conquer it.

The Aztec, or Mexica (May-SHEE-ka), had arrived in the fertile Valley of Mexico some time during the 12th or 13th century. Their original homeland is unknown. A small tribe, they were repeatedly rejected by the valley's inhabitants and were eventually chased into one of the five lakes in the valley, Lake Texcoco. There, in 1325, they settled on an island that they called Tenochtitlán.

Known to be fierce and resourceful warriors, the Mexica offered their military services to Azcapotzalco, the most powerful of the three city-states surrounding their island. They developed other political alliances by arranging marriages between their leaders and the daughters of nearby rulers. Thus they established themselves as legitimate residents of the valley and were included in trade exchanges, bartering fish and marine animals for building materials and other necessary goods.

The Aztecs ambush Cortés and his Tlaxcalan allies on one of the causeways leading to the mainland cities. Casualties were so high that the incident is known as the Noche Triste, or "Sorrowful Night."

The Mexica erected a permanent temple to their most important god, Huitzilopochtli. They constructed three causeways, or bridges, across the lake to allow foot access to and from the city. They also built aqueducts—waterways that carried fresh spring water directly to the city's inhabitants.

The inhabitants of Tenochtitlán developed many of the social trappings and physical conveniences that we consider original to our own time: in addition to plumbing, irrigation, highways, and bridges, they had temples, public plazas, ball courts, marketplaces, and even suburbs, each with its own facilities. Citizens had specialized occupations, such as craftspeople, merchants, priests, government officials, engineers, architects, lawmakers, and poets.

By the 15th century, the Mexica had become a powerful military force with strong political and economic ties to other cities in the valley. In 1430, emerging victorious from a two-year war against some of the surrounding cities, they joined forces with their wartime allies, the Acolhuaca and the Tepaneca, forming a "Triple Alliance" whose combined military power conquered many of their neighbors and eventually forged the Aztec Empire.

The Aztecs developed a complex class system that included slave labor, and they practiced human sacrifice (for religious purposes) and warfare on a scale unequaled by any group before them. And they created some of the most magnificent works of art in the world. By the time the first Spaniards arrived, the population of Tenochtitlán was 150,000 to 200,000—making the Aztec capital one of the largest cities of its time.

Around 1509, the Aztecs began seeing disturbing and unusual omens. A huge flame appeared in the sky each night. The waters of Lake Texcoco became suddenly and inexplicably turbulent. A woman was heard at night, crying, "Oh my beloved sons, now we are about to go!" And many elders reported having violent and terrifying dreams, in which the entire city was destroyed and its people forced to flee.

For almost 10 years, the city's astrologers labored to interpret the omens but could not agree on their meaning. Then, around 1518, messengers from the coast reported seeing strange "mounds" on the ocean. Emperor Motecuhzoma Xocoyotzin ("Courageous Young Lord," commonly called Montezuma) speculated that these mounds might signal the return of Quetzalcoatl, the Great Plumed Serpent. According to Mexica mythology, the god had left Mexico several centuries earlier, vowing to return and reclaim his kingdom in the year One Reed, or 1519.

When Montezuma heard of Cortés's arrival in Mexico, he was convinced that the god Quetzalcoatl had returned. Unsure how to proceed, he wavered between submission and defiance. As the Spanish approached, the Aztec emperor tried to buy time with lavish gifts and promises of gold, jewels, fabric, exotic feathers, even sacrificial victims. He sent the gifts and promises with messages urging the Spanish to turn back. But Cortés, tantalized by the gifts, sent word that they would not retreat.

For weeks the Spanish advanced through harsh and punishing terrain. In each city the Spanish marched through, Cortés savagely battled the inhabitants, who in many cases had been ordered by their Aztec masters to attack the Spanish. Cortés learned that these people were greatly dissatisfied with their Aztec rulers, and he managed to convince tens of thousands of them to join his forces. On November 8, 1519, Cortés and his

400 men, with legions of native warriors, rode up to the gates of Tenochtitlán. They met no resistance. Instead, curious Aztecs watched in awe as the strange armored men gathered outside the city. The emperor was carried across one of the city's causeways on a golden litter encrusted with jewels. Montezuma greeted Cortés cordially.

But wealth and conquest were uppermost in the conquistador's mind. Though technically guests in the royal palace, Cortés and his men soon made Montezuma their prisoner in everything but name. The Aztec emperor, resigned to his fate, showed the Spanish his people's magnificent treasures and took them to see many of the sacred ceremonies, including human sacrifices. Bernal Díaz, Cortés's chronicler, recorded his first impression of their visit to the high temple and the sight of the huge idol of Huitzilopochtli:

> He had . . . monstrous and terrible eyes, and the whole of his body was covered with precious stones, and gold and pearls, and . . . was girdled by great snakes made of gold. In one hand he held a bow and in the other some arrows. . . . [He] had around his neck some Indians' faces and . . . hearts, the former made of gold and the latter of silver. . . . There were braziers, and in them [the Aztecs] were burning the hearts of three Indians whom they had sacrificed that day. . . . All the walls were so splashed and encrusted with blood that they were black, the floor was the same, and the whole place stank vilely.

Horrified, Cortés called the Aztec gods "devils." One day, Cortés became so disgusted by the human blood he saw in one of the Aztec temples that he smashed an iron bar against a stone idol. Relations between the Spanish and the Aztecs quickly deteriorated after this incident.

In May 1520, Cortés learned that Diego Velásquez had dispatched a well-armed force from Cuba to arrest him. Acting swiftly, he gathered most of his men and marched for the coast, leaving one of his officers, Pedro de Alvarado, in command of Tenochtitlán. After a surprise attack on the camp of Velásquez's soldiers, Cortés took their leader, Pánfilo de Narváez, captive and convinced the 900 men to join him. With these new recruits, he set out for Tenochtitlán.

He returned to discover that the city was in armed revolt against his troops, who, upon Alvarado's orders, had slaughtered 600 of its nobles during a religious ceremony. The streets were deserted. The Aztecs were preparing another attack.

On June 25, 1520, the Aztecs swept down on the Spaniards from all sides. In the fierce battle that ensued, the Aztecs destroyed the three causeways linking the city to the mainland. The Spaniards were trapped. Desperately, they built a makeshift bridge over which they planned to steal out of the city during the night. But they were ambushed. Cortés lost more than half his men and as many as 3,000 Tlaxcalan allies; the number of Aztec casualties is unknown. Among the Spanish that night became known as the *Noche Triste*, or "Sorrowful Night."

By autumn of 1520, the Aztecs had a new emperor, the fierce Cuitláhuac, Montezuma's brother. And the Spanish had a new and unseen ally—disease. Within months, a smallpox epidemic swept through the native population, killing thousands. Cuitláhuac was among the first to succumb.

By June 1521, the Spaniards and their Indian allies laid siege to the Aztec capital. With deliberate, systematic ferocity, they proceeded to demolish the splendid city of Tenochtitlán, leaving no structure standing. Anyone found huddled within a building was killed. The surviving Aztecs had nothing but mud and brackish lake water to eat and drink. About 50,000 Indians starved to death; 250,000 were killed in battle.

By August 1521—less than two years after Cortés first arrived in Mexico—the Aztec Empire was reduced to rubble. The conquistador built a new city over the ruins of the old to prove to the remaining natives that they would never again rule. He called it Mexico City.

Cabeza de Vaca and his companions traveling westward across the unexplored plains of North America. The four survivors of the Narváez expedition reached the Gulf of California eight years after they began their journey. Their remarkable success was due in part to the friendly relations they established with native tribes along the way.

4

INTO THE
MAINLAND

Another early Spanish expedition ended far differently from that of Hernán Cortés. In 1528, a wealthy but foolhardy *hidalgo* (nobleman) named Pánfilo de Narváez, the man who had been sent to apprehend Cortés in Mexico, set sail with 400 men for the cape of Florida, landing near present-day Tampa Bay. As they pushed inland, the invaders, encumbered by their heavy European armor, soon found themselves hopelessly mired in swamplands and besieged by mosquitoes, hostile natives, alligators, and snakes. They retreated to the beach only to find that their ships were gone.

In makeshift boats made from local timber, they sailed along the coast of the Gulf of Mexico toward the Spanish colonies in Mexico. Storms, starvation, disease, and attacks by natives decimated the party. Narváez deserted them and was never seen or heard from again.

In fact, only four members of the original expedition were heard from again—but not until eight years later. One of the survivors was a black man, Estebanico de Dorantes, a Moorish slave of another of the four, the conquistador Andrés Dorantes. The third was Alonso de Castillo. And the fourth, destined to be best known and most celebrated, was a nobleman named Alvar Núñez Cabeza de Vaca.

When these weary, bedraggled, and bearded wanderers appeared near Culiacán on the west coast of Mexico in 1536, claiming to be survivors of the lost Florida expedition of Pánfilo de Narváez, they were immediately brought to the viceroy of New Spain, Antonio de Mendoza. Cabeza de Vaca and Estebanico told the viceroy a remarkable story of adventure and survival.

Natives try vainly to fight off attack dogs set upon them by de Soto and his men. One of the boldest and most capable of the conquistadors, de Soto was also among the cruelest—he was known to torture natives for minor offenses or solely for sport.

The makeshift boats had disintegrated along the Gulf of Mexico, and Cabeza de Vaca found himself marooned on the Texas coast near present-day Galveston, where he was enslaved by coastal natives. Determined to escape this area, "so remote and malign," Cabeza de Vaca headed west into unknown territory. In 1534, he met up with the three other survivors of the Narváez expedition.

Together they walked more than 1,200 miles, crossing scalding deserts, the Sierra Madre mountain range, and four rivers before reaching the Gulf of California in 1536.

The four men survived their perilous journey by befriending the various nomadic tribes of the regions that make up modern-day Texas and Mexico. Traveling and living with Native Americans,

continued on page 57

A CULTURE TRANSFORMED

A series of Chumash rock paintings, or pictographs, found in the hills of the tribe's southern California homeland. Many of these works of art are expressions of religious beliefs; others, such as the petroglyph on this book's cover, depict historic events in the lives of Native Americans.

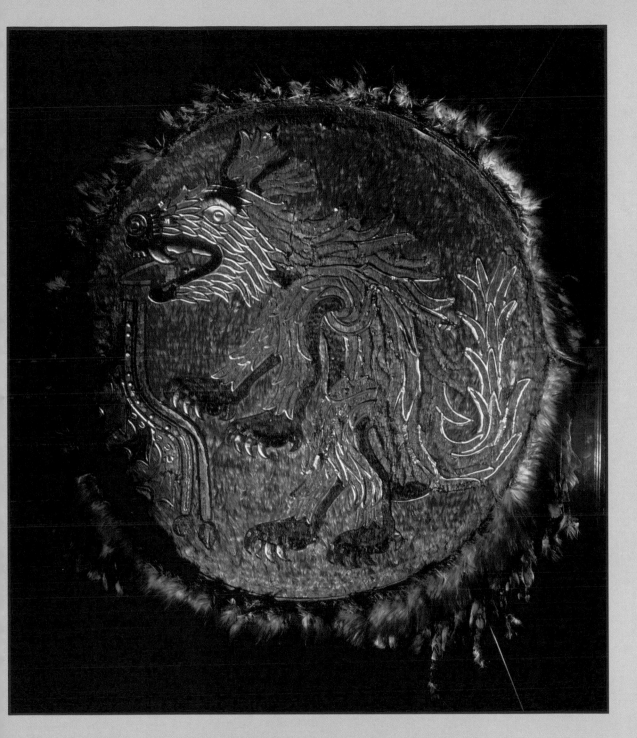

The magnificent feathered headdress (left) and shield (above) were believed to be among the gifts given by the emperor Montezuma to Cortés for the king of Spain. The emerald plumes of the priest's headdress, which measures nearly four feet high, are tail feathers from the quetzal and represent the sacred bird settling down from flight. The shield depicts the coyote, one representation of the Aztec fire god; the figure is outlined in pure gold, and the tufted border signifies flame.

This pectoral ornament, or pendant, was probably worn by an Aztec high priest or noble and may have been one of the treasures given to Cortés by Montezuma. Aztec stone-workers cut jade, pyrite, crystal, shell, and turquoise into tiny pieces and fitted them into knife handles, helmets, shields, skulls, and ornaments such as this double-headed serpent.

Like the pectoral ornament, this knife handle in the shape of a kneeling deity was formed with small pieces of turquoise and shell. The blade, which was used to cut out the hearts of sacrificial victims during Aztec religious rituals, would have been made of flaked chert and been extremely sharp.

One of the most significant events in Native American history, the introduction of the horse into North America by Spanish explorers, is graphically illustrated by this colorful beadwork bag fashioned by a modern Yakima craftsman.

This rawhide war shield, said to have been the property of the Oglala Sioux chief Crazy Horse, shows two horsemen confronting each other—a European with a rifle (left) and a Native American with a spear (right).

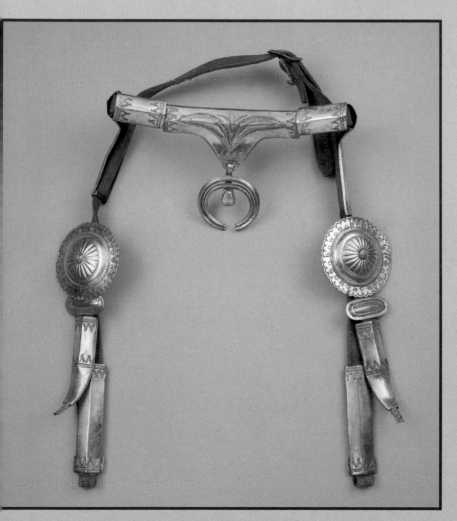

The first Native Americans to see Europeans on horseback were terrified by what they believed were half-man, half-beast creatures. By the 18th century, however, Native American tribes such as the Navajo, the Apache, and the Ute had begun raising their own herds and had become excellent riders. This Navajo silver headstall is an example of the finery that Native Americans often use to dress their mounts.

An above-ground beehive-shaped adobe oven in Taos Pueblo, New Mexico. This type of oven was introduced to Native Americans by the Spanish explorers.

continued from page 48

they wandered across southern Texas, moving gradually westward through lands that no non-Indian had ever seen. As Estebanico and Cabeza de Vaca learned the ways of the Native Americans, they also learned to respect them. Estebanico began to adopt their dress, assuming the trappings of a shaman, and both he and Cabeza de Vaca acquired reputations as healers, which helped to smooth their passage among the Southwest tribes. Finally, after eight years, Cabeza de Vaca and Estebanico encountered Europeans once again.

After a triumphant return to Spain in 1537, Cabeza de Vaca published an account of his harrowing journey. Despite candid descriptions of hunger, heartache, fatigue, harsh climates, hostile Indians, and other horrifying details, the public was excited by his reappearance and his tale. His 1542 account remains a classic of exploration and Native American anthropology.

The fierce native resistance that Ponce de León and Hernández de Córdoba had encountered on their forays into Florida and the disappearance of the Narváez expedition temporarily dampened Spanish interest in Florida. But the thirst for wealth and power was revived in 1533, after Francisco Pizarro invaded and conquered Peru. Pizarro's chief military officer, Hernando de Soto, returned to Spain with an enormous fortune and a burning ambition for more. Taking over the vacated rights of Narváez, de Soto assembled a fleet and crew and sailed for the New World—just after Cabeza de Vaca had returned to Spain, lucky to be alive.

Described by one chronicler as an "inflexible man, and dry of word," the conquistador Hernando de Soto was cruel as well. He was known to torture natives for sport; he brought with him on expeditions a pack of powerful and savage wolfhounds, greyhounds, and mastiffs and would often throw captive Indians to the dogs to be torn to pieces. One native was burned alive before his tribesmen because he refused to reveal the hiding place of his chief; when other tribe members stood firm, de Soto burned them too. He cut off hands, feet, and noses to punish minor offenses. At times he even sentenced his own followers to hanging or beheading if he believed it would improve discipline.

But de Soto was also a bold and capable leader. With a force much smaller than that of previous Spanish expeditions, his company traveled some 3,000 miles through inhospitable and almost completely unexplored territory: from Florida to North Carolina and Tennessee, through Alabama and Mississippi, into Arkansas, Oklahoma, and Texas, and then back to Arkansas before traveling down the Mississippi River to Mexico.

And he was better prepared than previous commanders had been. To prevent the threat of starvation that had plagued other expeditions, de Soto took with him 13 tough, long-legged hogs and bred them throughout the march, so that by the time the expedition reached the Mississippi River the men had hundreds of pigs to feast on. It is believed that the vicious wild hogs of the Okefenokee Swamp, known as

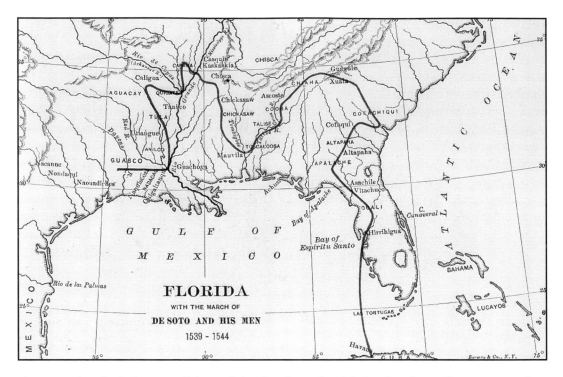

A map tracing the de Soto expedition and showing the various Native American tribes encountered along the route.

"piney woods rooters," are descendants of pigs that escaped de Soto's herd and grew larger and more savage on the abundant vegetation of the South.

De Soto also enlisted the services of craftsmen such as tailors, shoemakers, a farrier to shoe the horses, caulkers to seal boat seams, and a sword cutler. He brought with him a huge store of food in addition to the pigs, as well as 230 cavalry horses. For cooperative natives, he brought gifts of mirrors and beads; for hostile ones, he had iron collars.

In May 1539, de Soto made landfall near present-day Tampa—where the Narváez expedition had touched ground—and called it Espíritu Santu (Holy Spirit). The army marched inland and settled in an abandoned village. Meanwhile, de Soto sent out scouting parties to round up natives to use as interpreters and guides.

The Spaniards encountered a number of villages whose natives had fled upon hearing of the approaching army. Here, the men simply helped themselves to all available foodstuffs. Where de Soto did encounter Indians, he tried to bargain with them, but he met with hostility and suspicion; the Spanish reputation for brutality had preceded him. Often, the natives simply fabricated tales of riches and gold in other regions to entice the Europeans to leave their territory.

More than a month later, de Soto learned about Narváez's travails with the Apalachee. Crossing the Suwannee and Aucilla rivers, following Indian trails out of the country of the Timucua (the tribe whom Ponce de León had encountered), his men marched north into Apalachee territory. A scouting company came upon the bay where the ill-fated Narváez expedition had camped. They found the charcoal of his forge, wooden mangers, and the skulls of horses.

The following spring, the Spaniards journeyed eastward, where they were told they would find a marvelous land of riches, ruled by a female chief. To the Spaniards, the villages of the Florida Native Americans had all looked similar, but as they marched into present-day Georgia, they noticed changes. Instead of grass roofs, they saw cane. As with other Native Americans of the Southeast culture area, the Creek—so named by later English traders because they lived near woodland rivers and creeks—owned two houses per family, one for winter, plastered with clay and heated by fire "like an oven," and one for summer, located near a kitchen where corn bread was baked.

Each Creek family planted and tended its own garden, growing corn, beans, squash, pumpkins, melons, and sweet potatoes. All tribe members also worked in a communal field and contributed to a village store of provisions that fed warriors, guests, and the poor.

They supplied the Spaniards with turkey, partridges, and maize.

De Soto and his men were the first Europeans the Creek had ever seen. The Spaniards were impressed by the neatness and ingenuity of the natives' buildings and villages and by the tall physique, proud bearing, and distinctive dress of the Creek: the men wore colorful, dyed deerskins and the women wore skirts of bark or nettle grass.

With the help of Creek guides, de Soto reached Cofitachequi, about 25 miles below present-day Augusta, Georgia, where he met the amiable Creek *cacica*, or female chief, "quite graceful and at her ease," according to one of de Soto's chroniclers. Her stately conduct inspired the Spanish, who were often less than chivalrous toward Indian women, to call her La Señora de ("the Lady of") Cofitachequi.

La Señora offered provisions, canoes, and clothing to the Spaniards and presented de Soto with her own necklace, a "large strand of pearls as thick as hazelnuts which encircled her neck three times and fell to her thighs." De Soto, in turn, gave her a gold-and-ruby ring from his finger to indicate the kind of treasures they wanted. Though the natives gave them what they had—copper and slabs of shiny iron pyrite—the Spaniards were unsatisfied. By robbing the tribe's graveyard, they discovered more than 350 pounds of carved freshwater pearls, somewhat discolored by burial and fire (the Creek removed pearls from oyster shells by heating them).

The Creek cacica known as Le Señora de Cofitachequi presents de Soto with her pearl necklace. Native Americans frequently offered such items as gifts; the Spanish would give similar items in exchange to indicate the kind of treasures they were seeking.

Finally, the thievery perpetrated by the Spanish proved beyond the tolerance of the gracious La Señora, who refused de Soto guides or porters (natives who were pressed into service to carry the Spaniards' equipment). Undaunted, de Soto simply arrested and kidnapped her. She later escaped when the party arrived at the foot of the Blue Ridge Mountains.

The expedition entered Cherokee territory shortly afterward. Like the Creek, who probably gave them their name—calling them *tciloki*, or "people of the different speech"—the Cherokee lived along rivers and streams, where they cultivated beans, gourds, sunflowers, tobacco, and three different kinds of corn for roasting, boiling, and grinding into flour. In addition to edible roots, berries, fruits, and nuts, the Cherokee also subsisted on various kinds of fish. They were skilled hunters as well; deer and bear provided meat and skins for clothing and housing.

The Cherokee also had summer and winter houses. They practiced basket weaving, pottery making, and wood and stone carving, including the creation of booger masks, faces carved to represent evil spirits. And, like other Southeastern Indian tribes, they observed a number of hunting, farming, and healing rituals. One of the most important was the annual Green Corn Ceremony, which marked the beginning of the new year, after the last corn crop ripened in late summer.

Tribe members made elaborate preparations for the ritual. Men repaired the communal buildings while women cleaned their houses and cooking

A Native American priest prepares to consume the "Black Drink" before a gathering of warriors. Southeastern natives drank this mixture to purify their bodies and spirits before going to war or engaging in tribal rituals.

utensils, burned some possessions, and extinguished hearth fires. The most important villagers—chiefs, shamans, elders, and warriors—fasted. Those who had fasted then gathered for a feast of corn and the lighting of the Sacred Fire. They drank the "Black Drink," a ceremonial tea made from a poisonous shrub called *Ilex vomitoria*, tobacco, and herbs. The Black Drink induced vomiting and was thought to cleanse and purify the body. Some danced the Green Corn Dance as well.

Then the rest of the villagers joined in the ceremony by taking coals from the Sacred Fire to relight their hearth fires. An even bigger feast was prepared, and games and contests took place. All transgressions except murder were forgiven. The ceremony ended when the entire tribe took a communal, purifying bath in the river.

Another important event for the Southeastern Indians was the game of lacrosse. The object of the game was to toss a leather ball between posts using sticks with curved and webbed pockets. Though players could not touch the ball with their hands or use the sticks to fight, they could do just about anything else, including poking, bumping, stomping, and tripping one another. Not surprisingly, the games resulted in numerous injuries and some deaths.

The game was played between clans of the same or different tribes; sometimes huge matches took place between villages, with hundreds of participants. Ceremonies filled with dancing and singing preceded these events. Villagers placed bets and medicine men "coached" teams with incantations rather than strategy.

With Cherokee assistance, the de Soto expedition passed through "a high range" with "rough and lofty ridges"—the Great Smoky Mountains, or the southern end of the Blue Ridge—and exited the highlands at the Tennessee River, becoming the first Europeans to cross the Appalachian Mountains. Not until well into the next century would explorers again venture into this part of the Southeast.

In August 1540, the expedition entered Choctaw country, where they met the powerful chief Tascaluza. When de Soto demanded slaves, Tascaluza promised him 100 women as soon as the expedition reached Mauvilla (present-day Mobile). The Mauvillans, meanwhile, were preparing for battle. Against the advice of his scouts, de Soto led a vanguard into town, arriving on the morning of October 18, 1540. After rude treatment by de Soto, Tascaluza responded with defiance, prompting one of the Spanish soldiers to strike a native. Suddenly, thousands of Choctaw poured from their homes, screaming and firing arrows. Most of the panicked Spaniards managed to escape through the village gate.

De Soto quickly called for reinforcements and organized an assault. Squads of soldiers attacked the Choctaw fortress from all sides, setting fire to houses and driving the villagers out onto the plain, where the surrounding cavalry dispatched them as the infantry

Nineteenth-century artist George Catlin's painting of a Choctaw man named Drinks-the-Juice-of-the-Stone wearing the traditional dress of a lacrosse, or istaboli, *player. Often played in conjunction with tribal ceremonies, lacrosse matches sometimes involved entire villages or tribes and included hundreds of participants.*

charged through the gate. The Choctaw resisted ferociously; some even immolated (burned) or hanged themselves rather than submit to the invaders.

By day's end, 2,500 Choctaw were dead and their village was destroyed. Twenty-two Spaniards had died and 150 to 200 others, including de Soto, had been wounded. Over 80 horses and most of the Spaniards' possessions—clothes, food, pearls, medicine—had been destroyed by fire. One account says that the company dressed their wounds "with the fat of dead Indians."

Fearful of Native American reactions to the conquistador's death, the followers of de Soto bury his body in the Mississippi River.

Shortly after the battle, de Soto received word that his ships were only a six-day march away. But the conquistador knew that if his expedition returned to Spain in this condition—battered, hungry, wounded, and without treasure—his reputation would be ruined and he would never be able to muster a second expedition to Florida. He decided to keep moving.

In November 1540, the weary explorers reached Chickasaw territory in northeastern Mississippi and settled in an abandoned town of 200 huts.

De Soto tried to win the cooperation of the displaced cacique and his chiefs by sharing a feast of pork with them, but the Native Americans grew so fond of the meat that they began raiding the Spanish encampment for pigs. De Soto killed two of the poachers and severed the hands of a third, sending him back to the village as a warning.

Before dawn one morning, four months after the Spanish had settled there, the Chickasaw attacked, whooping and sounding noisemakers as they fired flaming arrows into the village. In the confusion, few Spaniards had time to find their weapons or mounts; they were saved only because the natives believed their stampeding horses to be a cavalry charge. The Chickasaw withdrew. One week later, they attacked again, but this time the Spanish were prepared, and they routed the Indians. Finally, in April 1541, the ragged army moved on, greatly reduced in number.

De Soto no longer seemed to have a fixed destination in mind; instead, warfare and plundering had become ends in themselves. In the village of Quizquiz, the marauding Spaniards seized 300 women for concubines. That day or the next, around the 8th of May, the Spaniards came upon the Mississippi, which they named the Rio Grande (Great River). The chronicler Rodrigo Ranjel described the river as "near half a league" (about a mile and a half) wide; so wide, he said, that a man standing on the opposite shore "could not be told, whether he were a man or something else."

But the explorers had little idea of the magnitude of their discovery. The Mississippi River is the world's third-longest waterway, after the Nile and the Amazon. Though a 1519 expedition and the 1528 exploration of Narváez had been there earlier, de Soto is generally credited with having first sighted the mighty river.

The Spaniards built four large rafts to ferry themselves and their equipment and horses across the river. Once on the Arkansas side of the river, they discovered a number of fortified native towns with "many skulls of bulls, very fierce" (these were probably buffalo heads) hanging above ceremonial buildings. The skins of deer, panther, and bear obtained from local natives were used to replace their tattered clothing, and the soldiers made new armor for their horses out of shields made of cowhide.

The Spaniards continued westward. By this time, the explorers—even the indefatigable de Soto—were weary of their expedition, and the commander was ailing from what was probably malaria or typhoid. So, in March 1542, they turned back and headed southeast toward the Mississippi, hoping to settle for the winter in what is now Georgia.

Through heavy snow and dangerous swamps, the Spaniards marched until they reached the Mississippi River again, at Guachoya. There they became enmeshed in native tribal wars, where one chief's insolence led de Soto to massacre 100 men and imprison 80 women and children.

On May 21, 1542, the conquistador died. Grief-stricken and frightened, the Spaniards buried de Soto's body that night without a marker, to hide the loss of their leader. But after the natives grew suspicious of his absence, the Spaniards dug up the body, weighted it down, and sank it in the Mississippi River. Then they moved on.

From June to October, the party journeyed westward, crossing the Red River near Shreveport, Louisiana, southwest into the Texas plains, where the expedition at last halted. Luis Moscoso, who succeeded de Soto as leader of the group, called a conference. Provisions were scant (they had lost most of their pigs) and winter was approaching. The desert described by Cabeza de Vaca lay ahead. The men agreed to return to the Mississippi River and try to sail down it into the Gulf of Mexico.

The desperate adventurers retraced their steps across territories that they had pillaged on their way out. Exposure, hunger, and exhaustion killed many Spaniards and nearly all of their Indian captives. Like the members of the Narváez expedition, they constructed boats with which to navigate the river. In July 1543, the survivors of the expedition—about half of the 600 who had landed four years earlier—boarded their seven makeshift boats and cast off.

Along the way, the Spanish behaved no better than they had on land. Each time they put to shore, the soldiers would steal grain, and when the natives objected, they torched their villages. They were harassed by outraged Native Americans for almost the entire length of the Mississippi. Finally, in late 1543, the bedraggled army of 311 reached Mexico City, where they disbanded. What had begun as a great dream of colonization and wealth had ended in a bloody rampage across the Southeast.

The entrance to the courtyard of a Catholic church at the Taos pueblo in New Mexico. Many of the churches established in the Southwest by 16th- and 17th-century Spanish missionaries still stand today.

5

BODIES
AND SOULS

While Hernando de Soto was tracing a path of destruction and conquest through the Southeast, another conquistador was making his way north from Mexico: Francisco Vásquez de Coronado. Born to a noble Spanish family, Coronado had followed Antonio de Mendoza, the viceroy of New Spain, to Mexico in 1535.

At this time, Europe and the New World were blazing with excitement over the reappearance of Cabeza de Vaca and his comrades. Until the four survivors of the Narváez expedition surfaced near the Gulf of California telling tales of prairies and deserts, high plateaus and rugged mountain ranges, great rivers and escarpments, and large, horned, shaggy beasts, Europeans had no idea of the vastness and natural wealth of North America.

Upon hearing Cabeza de Vaca's story, Mendoza began making plans for a massive *entrada*, or expedition, into the interior of the continent. In 1539, he

sent a scouting party led by a Franciscan missionary, Fray Marcos de Niza, with Estebanico de Dorantes as guide. Fray Marcos returned from his expedition several months later with a tale as horrifying as it was thrilling. They had indeed discovered a region of great wealth and beauty, which they called the Seven Cities of Cíbola. But the Zuni—a branch of the southwest Pueblo Indians whose cities Estebanico had entered—had killed the black explorer and cut him to pieces for an unknown offense.

Undaunted by the tragedy, Coronado left Mexico on February 22, 1540, with 337 soldiers, mostly mounted; 700 Native American servants, scouts, guides, and herdsmen; black servants; Franciscan priests; and large herds of horses, cattle, and sheep. Coronado led an advance party from Culiacán in Mexico to Hawikuh, a Zuni village in west central New Mexico. Along the

Coronado and his men cross the vast plains of the Midwest in their search for the Seven Cities of Cíbola. Though they never discovered the fabled region, members of a scouting expedition under one of Coronado's captains became the first Europeans to enter present-day California.

way, the Spaniards heard a message the Zuni had sent to outlying tribes. If the Spanish passed their way, the Zuni said, "they should not respect them, but kill them, for they were mortal." They had proof of this in the bones of Estebanico. As with the Aztecs and Cortés, the Zuni at first believed Estebanico to be a divine being and thus immortal.

The Zuni were expecting the Spanish to return to Hawikuh and avenge Estebanico's death, so they were ready for battle when Coronado and his men arrived in early July 1540. But Native American weapons were no match for the Spaniards, who were armored and on horseback, using "canes that spit fire and made thunder." The Europeans took

Hawikuh. The ancient culture of the Pueblo would be forever changed.

The Pueblo had descended from the Anasazi and Mogollon peoples of about 100 B.C. to A.D. 1300. They occupied the Colorado Plateau, Arizona, western New Mexico, and a 130-mile stretch of the Rio Grande that flows through most of the Southwest to the Gulf of Mexico.

Within the Pueblo tribe were four groups, each with a language of its own. The Pueblo lived in villages situated atop mesas (small plateaus).

The unique living arrangements of the Pueblo set them apart from other Native American cultures. Their homes, in villages also known as pueblos, were constructed much like modern apartment buildings, with stones that were mortared and surfaced with plaster, or with adobe bricks of sun-dried earth and straw. Each complex of several homes could be up to five levels high; the flat roof of one level was also the floor and front yard of another. To help fend off attacks, the walls of the ground floor had no windows or doors; instead, inhabitants climbed up ladders to enter through holes in the roofs.

The Pueblo cultivated multicolored corn, squash, beans, sunflowers, cotton, and tobacco. They raised domesticated turkeys and hunted wild deer, antelope, and rabbits. Pueblo men and women wore cotton, deerskin, or rabbitskin clothing and leather sandals or moccasins. Women created beautiful pottery by coiling, polishing, and painting clay. Men made carved wooden masks for elaborate religious ceremonies, including those that were believed to bring rain, essential for their livelihood.

Coronado was greatly disappointed by the modest appearance of the tribe. "I can assure you," Coronado wrote Mendoza, "that [Fray Marcos] has not told the truth in a single thing that he said, but everything is the opposite of what he related." They were impressed, however, with the Zuni's agricultural and architectural skills and their system of government, in which villagers followed the counsel of their oldest men.

Coronado dispatched lieutenants to explore the surrounding provinces. Word had quickly spread among Pueblo tribes that "Cíbola had been conquered by very fierce men who rode animals that ate people," and reactions to these Spanish forays were mixed. Some came to Hawikuh to offer friendship and gifts to the strangers. Others, such as the Hopi and the Acoma, gravely warned the Spaniards to stay away, but their resistance gave way when faced with displays of Spanish might.

Coronado traveled eastward to the province of Tiguex and displaced the Tiwa, another Pueblo tribe, from their 12 villages. The Tiwa ultimately rebelled, but the uprising was brutally crushed and many natives were burned alive. Finally, in an attempt to regain their territory, they resorted to trickery: an Indian captive was persuaded to tell fantastic tales of his native home in the east across the Great Plains, where even common "pitchers, dishes, and bowls were made of gold."

Enthralled, Coronado led his forces into what is now Kansas. But they found only an ocean of grass. None of them had seen anything like it before. Overwhelmed by the seemingly endless flatness, Coronado wrote that there was "not a stone, not a bit of rising ground, not a tree, not a shrub, not anything." They returned to Pueblo territory and remained there for the winter.

Coronado's reconnaissance teams discovered numerous wonders, including the Grand Canyon, the Colorado River, and a "race of giants" who turned out to be the tall, strong Yuma tribe. One scout, Captain Melchior Díaz, led his men across the Mojave Mountains; they were the first Europeans to enter present-day California. There, they

A village of the Acoma in New Mexico as it appeared in 1912, displaying the multilevel communal dwellings of the Pueblo tribes.

were astonished to find hot springs and mud volcanoes, "like something infernal."

But they discovered no gold and no riches. In 1542, Coronado ended his entrada and returned to Mexico empty-handed and disillusioned. He died in 1554, at age 44, of a head injury he had sustained on the expedition.

After this disappointing expedition, Spain financed no more entradas. The conquistadores had found no gold or silver on their inland journeys; more-over, Spain was intent on solidifying its control over Mexico. Only the Franciscan missionaries who had taken part in the entradas felt differently. To them, the

Zuni women tend a waffle garden near the banks of the Zuni River in 1911. The distinctive shape of the waffle garden helps conserve precious irrigation water in the arid climate of the Southwest.

Southwest harbored a multitude of pagan souls waiting to be converted to Christianity. While the bold horsemen dispersed, the friars plodded back into the region on mules or on foot, in the hope of establishing permanent missions in the Southwest.

Spanish missionaries had arrived in the New World years before: six Catholic priests were among Columbus's second crew in 1493. And when the first Franciscan missionaries arrived on the shores of Mexico in 1523, Hernán Cortés knelt and kissed the hems of their robes.

Although Christian ideals would seem to be at odds with the Spaniards' brutal treatment of the Indians, it must be remembered that Spanish Catholicism in the 16th century was a militant faith, shaped by hundreds of years of warfare. Conquistadores and missionaries alike believed that they were serving the natives well by bringing them the one true faith.

The spiritual emissaries to the New World acted, for the most part, out of genuine religious conviction. They were not looking for material wealth, as the conquistadores were, yet they faced many of the same perils. They ventured where these mighty horsemen would not go, or where they had failed to pacify the Native Americans they encountered.

Spain's interest in the development of missions in the New World was perhaps more practical than spiritual. The Spanish government believed that establishing missions among the native population offered the best and cheapest solution for holding on to territory. Spain's rulers reasoned that Indians who converted to Catholicism would be much less likely to attack Spanish colonies, whose residents were also Catholic. So, with Spain's encouragement, priests (and in some cases, nuns) lived among the Native Americans and labored to convert them to Catholicism. These conversions were more than mere professions of faith, however; to truly become a Christian, a Native American had to leave his or her tribe and village and adopt the ways of the European pioneers. Often, they paid with their

lives: diseases brought by Europeans spread even more quickly in missionary settlements.

When gentle persuasion failed, the Spanish used force to relocate Native Americans to mission settlements. Often they resorted to beating the natives and destroying their temples to hasten conversion. But some missionaries came to truly love and care for the natives among whom they lived and took up their cause, even when doing so meant defying the Spanish crown or the colonial government. Bartolomé de Las Casas, for example, the 16th-century "apostle to the Indies" who was the first priest ordained in the New World, worked tirelessly to draw attention to the horrible mistreatment of Indians. In 1542, his efforts paid off with the passage of the New Laws of the Indies, which ended the encomienda system.

Though the new ruling was intended to protect the natives of the Americas, it would have dire consequences for millions of people on another continent. To replace Native American laborers, Las Casas suggested Europeans or Africans. Spain approved its first direct shipment of slaves from Africa to the Americas in 1518: 4,000 Africans, almost 20 times the largest previous shipment, were transported to the New World.

Spain was not the only nation in Europe to seek dominion over the New World. In 1497, Great Britain sent an Italian mariner, John Cabot, to explore the northeast coast of America, and in the 1560s the English attempted a number of raids on the Spanish Caribbean. But

Bartolomé de Las Casas, the "apostle to the Indies," earned the respect of Native Americans by working to abolish the encomienda system in the New World.

Britain was unable to establish a substantial presence in the New World until 1607, when three small ships made landfall on the banks of the James River in Virginia and founded the settlement of Jamestown.

The French, too, had been trading in the Americas from the beginning of the 16th century. Their first official expedition, led by the Florentine navigator Giovanni da Verrazano, sailed in 1524. Verrazano explored the east coast of North America from the Carolinas to Nova Scotia, searching in vain for a passage to Asia. Two more expeditions, in 1534 and 1535–36, led by Jacques Cartier, would establish a French colony called Charlesbourg-Royal on the St. Lawrence River (near the present-day city of Québec). Like the English, the French would attempt to penetrate the Spanish stronghold in the tropics; they established bases on three small islands (Bermuda, St. Christopher, and Barbados) before the end of the 17th century.

Following their successful revolt against Spanish rule in Europe, the Dutch also became seafarers to the New World. Dutch fleets were often welcomed at trading ports of Portugal, which was also chafing under Spanish dominion, and thus they were able to establish a significant commercial presence, both in the tropics and in northeastern America.

Spain, meanwhile, did not attempt permanent colonization in the interior Southwest until several decades after Coronado's ill-fated expedition. In 1598, a wealthy Spanish noble named Juan de Oñate led a caravan deep into present-day New Mexico and established a small settlement near the pueblos of the Rio Grande. In 1610, Pedro de Peralta replaced Oñate as governor and moved the colony farther south. This settlement, originally called La Villa de Santa Fe, would eventually become the foremost Spanish city in New Mexico.

For the next 70 years, settlers arrived and the Santa Fe colony grew— but it did so at the expense of the Navajo, Apache, and other Native American tribes living there. After years of ill treatment, enslavement, and punishment for refusing to convert to Christianity, these local tribes began raiding the Spanish settlements.

In 1680, the Pueblo, led by a Tiwa shaman called Popé and aided by the Apache, carried off a massive revolt against the Spanish in New Mexico. In the Pueblo Rebellion, as it is called, hundreds of Spaniards were killed and the entire Spanish population was driven from the region. But the Native American victory was short-lived. In 1693, New Mexico governor Diego de Vargas marched north from El Paso and recaptured Santa Fe in bloody battle. Eighty-one Indians died in the fighting. Vargas ordered the execution of another 70, and 400 more were taken captive.

The Spaniards soon learned of a new threat to their settlements, however. The Indians, once terrified of horses, were now raising their own herds—the offspring of horses stolen from the Spanish—and they had become excellent riders. The Spaniards had lost one of their greatest advantages over the natives. The Ute, the Navajo, and the Apache began swooping down on Spanish settlements and terrorizing the colonists.

As a result of this mounted resistance, Spanish colonization slowed during the 18th century. Only the intrepid missionaries dared to venture into the Southwest. One of the best known of these pioneers was the zealous Spanish monk Junípero Serra.

Born to hardworking peasants on the Spanish island of Majorca, Serra became a Franciscan when he was just 18, and in 1748, he traveled to Mexico as a missionary. Twenty years later, in June 1767, Spanish officials there enacted the first of several edicts issued by King Charles III that would eventually result in the expulsion of the Jesuits (the members of the religious order called the Society of Jesus) from all Spanish territory in the New World and ultimately from Spain itself. Serra was sent to the long, desolate peninsula known as Baja California to take over the missions formerly run by the Jesuits.

The first of 21 Jesuit missions on the peninsula had been established in 1697 by the missionary Juan María Salvatierra. Although the Spanish found Baja California forbidding and desolate, it supported a large number of Native Americans: the Jesuits estimated their number at 40,000 when they first arrived. California peoples were primarily nomadic hunter-gatherers who subsisted on wild plants, such as berries, nuts, seeds, greens, roots, bulbs,

and tubers. They also ate insects: they picked grubs and caterpillars off plants and boiled them in salt, and they drove grasshoppers into pits, then roasted them. They hunted deer, rabbits, ducks, geese, and swans and caught fish with hooks, spears, and nets.

The Baja natives, who were described by Junípero Serra and other missionaries as handsome people, wore almost no clothing in the torrid climate of the Baja. Men usually went naked or wore simple breechcloths; women wore fringed aprons in the front and back, made from animal skins or shredded bark. After the Europeans arrived, the Native Americans began wearing cotton garments made from imported fabric. Many went barefoot, but some wore moccasins of leather or sandals made of plant fiber. They wore shell jewelry and tattooed their skin.

To his dismay, Junípero Serra discovered that the Jesuit missions were in astonishingly bad condition. Moreover, Native Americans had been driven from their own lands, transferred en masse to distant regions of the peninsula, and forced to mingle with members of unfamiliar tribes. As a result of these upheavals, the Native American birthrate in the region plunged. European epidemics of tuberculosis, smallpox, syphilis, and measles had also killed off the Indians by the thousands. By the time Serra and his team of Franciscan missionaries arrived, the native population of the Baja had diminished by more than 80 percent, to just 7,000 people.

A painting depicting the simple dress and the village life of California Native Americans. Primarily hunter-gatherers, California peoples lived in crude, open-topped conical structures made of brush or reeds over a frame of willow poles. Such dwellings could be easily dismantled when moving from place to place.

An artist's depiction of the Spanish mission at San Diego, California, one of the many established by the Franciscan order under Junípero Serra.

Serra was not able to do much for the natives of the Baja, however. Almost as soon as the monk had arrived, José Gálvez, the inspector general for the region, began making plans to colonize the region that Spain called Alta California. (In Spanish, *alta* means "high" and *baja* means "low"; hence, Upper and Lower California, or the region that is today the state of California and the Baja Peninsula.)

Since Spain had little money or manpower, Gálvez's plan for the settlement of California relied on the dauntless Franciscan missionaries, particularly Junípero Serra, for its success. A small band of soldiers and priests traveled to San Diego, and then, after much hardship and suffering, Serra reached Monterey. In both places, he successfully established Franciscan missions.

From 1770 to 1783, Serra, his fellow priests, and Spanish soldiers, combining brutal force with gentle persuasion, carried on the work of converting California's Indians, whose numbers and variety were unmatched anywhere else in the lands that eventually became the United

States. Serra oversaw the establishment of nine more missions, including San Luis Obispo, San Francisco, San Juan Capistrano, and Santa Clara. The intrepid Spanish missionary died in 1784 from an unrecorded illness (possibly lung cancer).

Around the same time, Spain was sponsoring its last great inland expedition. In 1776, Fray Silvestre Vélez de Escalante, a 25-year-old friar, set out to explore the unknown land between the Spanish outposts in New Mexico and those that had been established in California. His destination was Serra's Monterey mission.

On their 2,000-mile journey, Escalante and his men explored the western slopes of the Rocky Mountains and became the first white men to traverse the canyons of the upper Colorado River. They mapped numerous rivers and made contact with a dozen Native American tribes. Although they were prevented from reaching Monterey by foul weather, the exploring team mapped the area so well that generations of future pioneers—including the German explorer Alexander von Humboldt and the American explorer Zebulon Pike—relied on the Escalante maps to probe the American Southwest.

The Castillo de San Marcos in St. Augustine, Florida, was the first permanent settlement in what is now the United States and was the anchor of a string of Spanish military posts crossing the peninsula. Sacked in 1586 by the British, St. Augustine officially became British property in 1763, was returned to Spain in 1783, and became U.S. property when Spain ceded Florida in 1821.

6

THE STRUGGLE
FOR POWER

While Spanish missionaries traveled through the West and Southwest, the English and French were positioning themselves to gain control of the Southeast mainland. Although their methods differed, their goals did not. Each of the three European powers sought to outdistance its rivals by enlarging the boundaries of the New World territory under its control. To accomplish this, they formed alliances with native groups, obtained their trade, and incited them to war against their opponents or the Native American allies of their opponents. The alliances also served the interests of the Native Americans, who used their ties with the European powers as an excuse to settle old rivalries with other Indian groups. Ultimately, however, the Native Americans became entangled in the power struggle between the Spaniards, the British, the French, and, eventually, the Americans of the new United States.

After de Soto's ravages in Florida, Spanish missionaries and settlers faced violent resistance from Native Americans. But the peninsula's strategic location as a supply post to Havana and Veracruz was crucial. So in 1565, a Spanish commander named Pedro Menéndez de Avilés established a major mainland naval base and a number of garrisons and missions along the Atlantic coast to protect Spanish interests from Great Britain, which had taken control of the Carolinas, and France, which had settlements in Louisiana. The main Spanish stronghold was named St. Augustine, the first Spanish and the first permanent European settlement in the Southeast.

There, Spanish missionaries worked with the Timucua Indians, whom Ponce de León had encountered nearly 200 years earlier. Eventually, they developed an entire network of stations, stretching westward across the land to Apalachee country (Tallahassee).

A Seminole family wearing the typical clothing of the Florida Indians in the late 1800s.

By 1700, the Spanish had successfully fortified Florida against encroaching sovereignties. But their hold was short-lived: a few years later, the powerful Creek tribe, working with the English in the Carolinas, raided the settlements. All the missions were destroyed or abandoned, and the local natives were nearly annihilated in slave raids.

Over the next few decades, Spain formed alliances with some Creek bands and persuaded them to relocate to Florida as a buffer against the British, thereby curbing foreign incursions. By 1750, they had regained control of Pensacola, St. Marks, and St. Augustine, three important settlements in their network of missions and forts. But travel between St. Marks and St. Augustine was extremely hazardous: a new Indian group known as the Seminole, who had taken refuge in central Florida, was inhabiting and defending the land between the settlements.

Before Europeans arrived in Florida, it was populated mainly by two tribes: the Timucua of the north and the Calusa of the south. As the English gained ground in the Southeast and the Spanish fought to maintain their settlements, the Native Americans of this region became enmeshed in the struggle. Those who allied themselves with the British helped drive the Spanish southward; some even raided Spanish missions in Florida, using guns provided by their allies to kill unarmed natives. Because Spanish policy prohibited Native Americans from owning guns, members of the Timucua and Calusa were easily

captured and enslaved—either by colonists or other Indians—in Spanish-controlled areas. Many of the Florida natives who escaped death or capture fled to the Spanish islands. By the beginning of the 18th century, the Timucua and the Calusa were nearly extinct.

The entire Native American population of the Southeast was suffering massive dislocation and disorganization. The tribes living in English territory north of Florida often made war upon each other, as well as upon tribes farther south. Some of these rivalries were traditional; others were fostered by the English, who were eager to drive the natives out of the area and open it for European settlement. As a result of this turmoil, tribes grew even smaller in size and people were left homeless. Some fled to Spanish territory in Florida. Soon, other groups of Native Americans, including the Creek living near present-day Oconee, Georgia, settled in Spanish territory as well.

For a time, the territory dividing South Carolina and Florida (present-day Georgia) became a buffer zone between Spain and England, where many displaced Native Americans and escaped African slaves sought refuge. When Great Britain took possession of Georgia, however, these peoples moved farther south into Florida, where they were protected by Spanish laws and granted Spanish citizenship.

The Native Americans and blacks who migrated to Florida were called Seminole by the Europeans—probably a mispronunciation of the Creek word *simanoli*, meaning "a runaway," or "undomesticated," "wild." At first these groups spoke many different languages, but over time they began to favor two dialects, Muskogee and Mikasuki. By the 19th century, all other dialects had been forgotten.

Because the Seminole had no competition, and because the Spanish did not desire the land for settlement, they thrived in their new land. They acquired new crops like melons and oranges and were introduced to domesticated animals like horses, cows, and pigs. As refugees from the north continued to be absorbed into the tribe, the Seminole became more unified and cohesive.

In 1763, Spain was forced to relinquish Florida in exchange for Cuba, which the British had captured the previous year. At the same time, France transferred to Spain its portion of Louisiana, giving Spain the advantage of control over most of the coast from Texas to Georgia. Spain encouraged residents of Florida to leave the newly acquired British territory by offering lands and assistance to resettle on the "mainland" of Cuba. About 3,000 residents of Florida—Spanish, mulattoes, blacks, and Native Americans—left Florida for the Spanish islands.

Spain regained Florida in 1783, when Great Britain was defeated in the Revolutionary War. As a result of the Treaty of Paris, Great Britain ceded its former 13 colonies to the Americans. But Britain made no provisions for the Native Americans who had sided with it during the war. Britain's defeat and the subsequent formation of the United States ended the peace and prosperity of the newly formed Seminole.

During the 18th century, European immigrants streamed into America in increasingly greater numbers. America may have offered greater social freedom than Europe, but most Europeans were lured across the sea by the dream of owning land, which they associated with political and economic freedom.

The concept of individual land ownership was unknown to Native Americans, however. Among them, land was owned communally, by tribes or clans rather than by individuals. Even this communal ownership differed from the European notion of holding title to property: Native Americans saw themselves as sharing the land with other living things, not as masters of everything on the land. When villages, clans, or tribes fought over control of territory, they were contesting the right to live, farm, or hunt in a region, not the right to own the land itself.

In Florida, as elsewhere across the country, the American settlers began forcing their way into the territory and establishing farms. After repeated warnings, the Seminole began raiding the newcomers' homesteads.

The Seminole were further provoked when southern plantation owners started taking steps to prevent runaway African slaves from crossing the Florida border. The planters accused the Seminole of stealing their "property" and sent slave catchers into Florida to recapture the runaways, many of whom had become members of the tribe.

SEMINOLE RESERVATION ESTABLISHED UNDER TREATY OF 1823

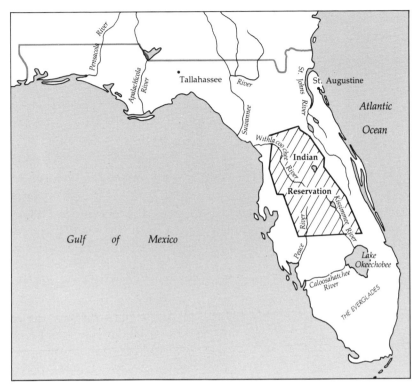

The Seminole reservation, established by treaty with the U.S. government in 1823, was 25 million acres smaller than the tribe's original territory and had no coastal access for trade.

Hostilities among other southeastern Native Americans did not help the cause of the Seminole. During the War of 1812 between Great Britain and the United States, Native Americans opposed each other as some sided with the United States and some with Britain. When a group of Creek captured an American army post near Mobile, Alabama, and massacred the inhabitants in 1813, the U.S. Army retaliated. In the war that followed (the Creek War of 1813–14), some Creeks allied themselves with the United States to fight against members of their own tribe. Scores of Native Americans died in the war, and in the end the Creek were forced to sign a treaty with the United States that ceded all Creek lands in Georgia and part of Alabama to the U.S. government. Rather than live under federal domination, many Creeks fled to Florida, where they were incorporated into the Seminole tribe.

With conflict between the Seminole and American settlers continuing, the U.S. government declared war on the Native Americans of Florida in 1817. Under the pretense of retrieving runaway slaves, federal troops marched into Spanish territory, burning and destroying Seminole property, land, and food. Both black and Indian members of the Seminole were taken as slaves. In

the fighting, later known as the First Seminole War, American troops under General Andrew Jackson subdued the tribe and drove the Spanish and the Seminole southward. Though the Seminole fought ferociously, they eventually retreated into the swamps and marshes of southern Florida, where capture was impossible.

In 1821, the Spanish territory of Florida, including the former Seminole land, was sold to the United States by treaty. Although federal control had passed to the United States, slaves continued to seek refuge with the Native Americans. But American settlers moving into Florida demanded the removal of all Indians from the territory, and in 1823, near St. Augustine, 70 Seminole chiefs met with Florida's governor to discuss removal. They refused to reunite with the Creek in Georgia but agreed to move onto a reservation farther south, in central Florida. Most of the chiefs signed the treaty, which promised the Seminole the right to lands where non-Indians were prohibited from hunting, trespassing, or settling. In

This 1939 painting by Elizabeth Janes depicts the Cherokee removal to Indian Territory, a long and brutal journey that became known as the Trail of Tears. Between 1830 and 1840, the Creek, Chickasaw, Seminole, and Choctaw tribes were also forced to relocate west of the Mississippi.

return, the Seminole agreed to stop harboring escaped slaves.

In return for 30 million acres of fertile farmland, the Seminole received approximately 5 million acres of land unfit for cultivation. The reservation soil was sandy and marshy, and the tribe was now inland and therefore effectively cut off from access to guns and ammunition. As subjects of Spain, the Seminole had land and citizenship. As subjects of the United States, they owned nothing, and they were not recognized as U.S. citizens.

The plight of the Seminole was not unique. Beginning in 1791, the United States had begun addressing the problem of a humane coexistence between Native Americans and the new Americans. But the resulting treaties often showed little tolerance for cultural differences. Like the Spanish and other European powers who colonized North America, the United States expected Native Americans to change their traditional ways of life and become more like whites. Time after time, treaties signed with the United States guaranteeing Native American

land rights were violated. The common belief among whites was that Native Americans did not "use the land"; that is, they did not extensively cultivate or establish settlements in the way that whites did. By the end of the 18th century, there were nearly 4 million people in the United States. By 1800, the population had grown to more than 5 million, and by the end of the 19th century it had swelled to nearly 76 million.

In 1830, Andrew Jackson, who had become president of the United States, convinced Congress to pass the Indian

Settlers camp near Santa Fe, New Mexico, in 1880. The Santa Fe Trail, the first commercial route to the West, was established in 1821.

Removal Act, which required all Native Americans living in the East and Southeast to cede their land to the government in exchange for land in unsettled territories west of the Mississippi River. Although some legislators who supported the bill believed it was the only way to ensure Native American survival, the enactment of the bill resulted in catastrophe for many Native American peoples.

Between 1830 and 1840, more than 50,000 natives—among them the Cherokee, Creek, Chickasaw, Seminole, and Choctaw tribes—were forced to abandon their homes and move to a region designated as Indian Territory (present-day Oklahoma). During their midwinter journey of 800 miles, the Cherokee alone lost at least 4,000 members to exposure and starvation on what would become known as the Trail of Tears. Some tribes, such as the Illinois Sauk and Fox and the Seminole, resisted relocation, but by the mid-1840s, nearly all the tribes that once inhabited the eastern United States had been forced to move west of the Mississippi.

Native Americans across the continent fared no better than those in the Southeast. Spanish missionaries in California had succeeded in turning the Native Americans into a labor force for a thriving agricultural base. The towns that developed around these missions had more contact with the outside world than traditional Native American villages had: British, American, and Russian ships regularly anchored in coastal towns to exchange manufactured goods for hides and timber.

In 1821, the Spanish colonial government removed restrictions on foreign trade in its New Mexico territory, thus paving the way for a commercial route to Missouri that became known as the Santa Fe Trail. In the next 10 years, at least three other trails were laid through the Southwest from Santa Fe to California. These routes opened up the West even further to foreign influence and permanently altered the lives and lands of Native Americans.

Also in 1821, Mexico declared independence from Spain and inherited New Spain's northern provinces of Alta California, Texas, and New Mexico —present-day California, Nevada, Utah, Colorado, Arizona, New Mexico, Texas, and parts of Wyoming—or what is today called the Southwest. The northernmost areas of this territory were barely affected by the revolution. But Texas, which was most accessible from and most dependent upon central Mexico, underwent great change.

For hundreds of years, the area of present-day Texas was home to richly varied Native American tribes: the nomadic, hunter-gatherer Kiowa, Comanche, and Apache of the arid western plains; the agricultural Waco of the central region and the Nacogdoche of the eastern pine woods; and the fishermen Karankawa of the Gulf Coast. One historian notes that "more tribes have lived in Texas during historic times than in any other state of the United States." Unfortunately, many of these were extinct before outsiders could learn anything more than their names, and others were surely gone long before that. The French explorer René-Robert Cavelier de La Salle noted in 1685 that 51 identifiable Indian nations were living in Texas. Less than 150 years later, another explorer, Jean Louis Berlandier, observed that of those named by La Salle, "scarcely three or four are known nowadays under the names [La Salle] gives them."

In Texas, as with the rest of the continent, Native American populations began to decline almost immediately after Europeans arrived in America. Many were wiped out by epidemics of cholera, smallpox, measles, and other diseases brought by the Europeans. Later, intertribal warfare and alliances with and against the Spanish, Mexicans, Texans, and citizens of the United States reduced their numbers even further. By the end of the 19th century, many Texas tribes—including the Teja, who gave their name to the state—had become or were about to become extinct; those who remained represented mere fragments of their original tribes. It was not until the beginning of the 20th century that the 400-year decline in Native American populations ceased and growth again began to occur.

This early-20th-century photograph shows Yakima chiefs posing in front of the Capitol in Washington, D.C., where they would confer with Congress on land rights.

7

CHANGING CULTURES

The Spanish conquest of the Americas is unlike any other conquest in human history in that it swept whole continents in a matter of decades. "In one generation the Spaniards acquired more new territory than Rome conquered in five centuries," historians Samuel Eliot Morison, Henry Steele Commager, and William E. Leuchtenburg write in *The Growth of the American Republic*.

The legacy of this conquest is not easily labeled, however. Whole civilizations were destroyed in the name of the Spanish crown and the Church. But Spain's representatives in the Americas —the explorers, the conquistadores, and members of the clergy—also tried to preserve many of the cultures and traditions they encountered in the New World. While contemporary historians and students continue to debate Spain's legacy, one fact is unquestioned: the Spanish presence in the Americas left the people and the landscape forever changed.

In its first contacts with the New World, the Spanish crown sought to establish a bi-level society in the Indies by instituting the encomienda, in which Indians were more or less wards of the state. This social structure was intended not only to protect the natives, but also to allow the Spanish to maintain order and effect change with relative ease (as with conversions to Christianity). But in reality, relationships between Native Americans and Spaniards were much more complex.

Though the richly developed agriculture of Native Americans remained the principal means of subsistence, Spanish crops, animals, and farming equipment gradually changed cultivating methods for good. The Spaniards imported wheat and barley and introduced European cattle, sheep, swine, horses, burros, and mules. They brought Andalusian plows, metal tools, and guns; they established sugar plantations, vineyards, and other horticultural enterprises. They created a

An ax head, a hoe, and an adze (carving tool) traded to the Creek by Spanish settlers in the 17th century. Durable iron implements and other European goods were highly sought after by the Native Americans of the region.

ranching industry, and where valuable metals were discovered, they established mining districts.

As sea traffic to the Americas increased, Spain and other European countries were faced with expanding commercial needs: more provisions for ships and settlements, more goods for trading, and new goods that had yet to be introduced to colonial economies. In the New World itself, a successful barter system evolved between natives and Europeans. Because the ordinary goods of one culture often seemed appealing and exotic to the other, both sides generally judged the exchanges highly profitable.

While some Spaniards learned a great deal about their new trading partners, many others cared little about the widely varying cultures and traditions of the Native Americans. Before the Spanish arrived in the New World, Native American communities varied widely in size and cohesion. The family was the primary social unit in most tribes; small groups of families often comprised an entire village. In some cases—as with the Iroquois of the Northeast–Great Lakes culture area—

these groups lived in communal homes. But there the similarities ended.

The peoples who came to be known as "Indians" were actually hundreds of different groups, each different from the next in language, territory, and tribal affiliation. As historian D. W. Meinig observes:

> What Europeans labeled as an Indian "nation" might vary from an independent band of a hundred people to a loose confederation of many thousands, and the record of two centuries of encounters along the North American seaboard produced such a variety of names that there remain many uncertainties about the actual participants and patterns of particular localities. One general fact is clear, and further complicates the matter: the impact of European contact was so disruptive as to cause major change in the location, affiliation, and identity of many indigenous groups, and these changes too, have been reported entirely through European interpreters.

Spanish colonization altered Native American life in many ways. Organization around municipalities, or political units, was unknown to the Native Americans. Physically, Spanish towns were constructed according to a standard European plan: a rectangular grid of streets and buildings around a central, communal plaza. Displaced Native Americans or those who had migrated to such towns made new associations with other tribes and native cultures. The degree to which Native Americans adopted European dress, culture, language, and customs varied widely among tribes as well.

Other forces also altered the Native American population. By the 17th century, a distinct Spanish-American culture had evolved in the New World. Continuous contact between Spaniards, Native Americans, blacks, and other Europeans produced peoples of widely varying heritages and cultural affiliations. Some of this blending occurred through cohabitation and marriage among Europeans, Native Americans, and blacks. However, millions of Native Americans—and later, Africans—were simply appropriated by Europeans as concubines and slaves.

As a result, these new communities included peoples of widely varying extraction, such as mestizos (of European and Native American ancestry) and mulattoes (of white and black ancestry). Even distinctions between those of pure Spanish descent born in Spain (*peninsulares*), those born on Spanish-held tropical islands (*isleños*), and those born in America (*criollos*) became important in defining social status.

In his demographic study, *American Indian Holocaust and Survival* (1987), Russell Thornton describes the complex system by which the Spaniards classified peoples of mixed blood:

> In the central and southern parts of the hemisphere, the Spanish *conquistadores* and those who followed them classified the offspring of Europeans and American Indians or Africans on the basis of *mestizaje* (literally, race mixture, or miscegenation); offspring of Europeans and Indians were *mestizo*, offspring of Europeans and Africans were *mulato*, offspring of

Africans and Indians were *zambo* (and a non-Indian who lived like an Indian was designated *indígena*). All of these groups were eventually further classified by an elaborate, complicated scheme to denote varying degrees of color admixture (*castas de mezcla*).

Thornton cites a list from 18th-century New Spain that graphically illustrates the meticulousness with which Europeans distinguished among mixed-blood people:

1. Spaniard and Indian beget mestizo.
2. Mestizo and Spanish woman beget castizo.
3. Castizo woman and Spaniard beget Spaniard.
4. Spanish woman and Negro beget mulatto.
5. Spaniard and mulatto woman beget morisco.
6. Morisco woman and Spaniard beget albino.
7. Spaniard and albino woman beget torna atrás.
8. Indian and torna atrás woman beget lobo.
9. Lobo and Indian woman beget zambaigo.
10. Zambaigo and Indian woman beget cambujo.
11. Cambujo and mulatto woman beget albarazado.
12. Albarazado and mulatto woman beget barcino.
13. Barcino and mulatto woman beget coyote.
14. Coyote woman and Indian beget chamiso.
15. Chamiso woman and mestizo beget coyote mestizo.
16. Coyote mestizo and mulatto woman beget ahí te estás.

A shy Indian girl is offered by her father to a European trapper in this painting by 19th-century artist Alfred Jacob Miller. The artist noted that the bride cost her future husband $600 worth of trade goods.

Despite the intermingling of cultures, the balance of power between the conquerors and the conquered remained fundamentally unchanged. Under the encomienda system, Spanish conquistadores replaced Indian nobles as lords of land and labor. After the decline of the encomienda system, landownership retained its importance as a designation of power and status. So colonists acquired property by any means possible—through royal land grants, purchase, or inheritance, or if necessary by taking the communal lands of Indian villages.

By the 18th century, large Spanish-owned estates—called *haciendas*—dominated the Spanish-American landscape. With less land of their own to farm, and unable to support their families, Native Americans again sought work from the Spaniards. The work was seasonal and they were poorly paid, but many Native Americans had little choice. They became indebted to the Spanish once again. This system of land distribution —which guaranteed power and status for the landowners and a life of misery for the workers—formed the basis of social tensions that have endured into the 20th century in Mexico and other parts of Latin America.

A social order driven by color and class added to the difficulties encountered by Native Americans. White Europeans (a group that includes Spaniards) stood at the top of the social order, while darker-skinned Indian peoples occupied the lower rungs. "Throughout the Americas the inferior status of Indians within the colonial . . . system left a legacy of racism and inequality that continues to plague its people," historian Peter Winn writes in *Americas: The Changing Face of Latin America and the Caribbean*.

Over time, the blending of populations has somewhat blurred these distinctions. In Mexico today, as in much of Latin America, a majority of the population consists of people with mixed-race ancestry. This racial mixing is still reshaping these societies.

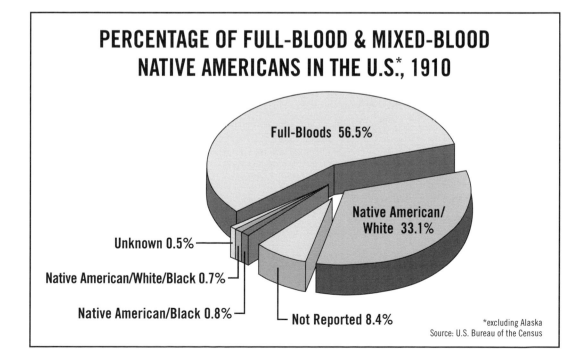

PERCENTAGE OF FULL-BLOOD & MIXED-BLOOD NATIVE AMERICANS IN THE U.S.*, 1910

Full-Bloods 56.5%

Native American/ White 33.1%

Unknown 0.5%

Native American/White/Black 0.7%

Native American/Black 0.8%

Not Reported 8.4%

*excluding Alaska
Source: U.S. Bureau of the Census

Five hundred years after Christopher Columbus, the question of what makes one Native American or Hispanic is still difficult to answer. Mexican Americans, such as politician Henry Cisneros (this page), are cultural descendants of Native American and Spanish ancestors; many Cuban Americans, such as entertainer Gloria Estefan (opposite page), are descendants of Native Americans, Spanish settlers, and the African slaves whom the Spanish brought to the island.

Race is also a defining factor for many population groups in the United States. A Native American is usually defined as having at least one-quarter Indian blood. Treaties between the U.S. government and Native American tribes commonly define what the government classifies as a Native American; some, such as the 1830 treaty with the Sauk and Fox, the 1865 treaty with the Blackfoot (which was never ratified), and the 1895 agreement with the Indians of Fort Belknap Indian Reservation in Montana, specifically refer to mixed-bloods as well. Treaty benefits were usually extended only to those mixed-bloods who followed tribal ways of life; those who lived nontraditionally were excluded. Unlike full-blooded Native Americans, mixed-bloods who were included were often given the choice of living tribally on reservations.

Racial mixing through intermarriage has also occurred in the United States.

In the U.S. Census report of 1910—the first to collect significant information on Native Americans of mixed blood—33 percent of the total Native American population in the United States was of Indian-white extraction (individual tribal percentages varied greatly). One of the reasons for intermarriage was survival: between 1890 and 1900, Native American populations had dropped to such low levels that they were nearly destroyed completely.

Moreover, as non-Indians have contributed to the American Indian population, the reverse has also been true: the 1980 U.S. Census recorded slightly fewer than 1.4 million Native Americans, but about 7 million Americans (Native American and otherwise) with some degree of Indian ancestry.

But the way in which Americans of European extraction view their heritage is significantly different from the way Native Americans view theirs. From the birth of the first mixed European–Native American child, Europeans sought to define such offspring according to social status. Native Americans had yet to view themselves as members of a broadly defined category like "American Indians," however; for them, the tribe was the primary social unit. For this reason, though they may have wondered whether such children were tribal members or Europeans, they probably never questioned whether mixed-blood children were Indian.

The question of what defines an American of Spanish descent is equally complex. A great percentage of the approximately 25 million U.S. citizens today who trace their origins to a region of the Spanish-speaking world can also claim Native American ancestry. To be "Hispanic" as defined by the U.S. Census Bureau, one "can be of any race." But many of those included in this broad category prefer to be known by other names. The way in which one defines oneself often implies not only a specific set of loyalties or affiliations, but also a certain way of seeing oneself. A person born in Texas of parents who came from Mexico, for example, might view himself primarily as Mexican, Mexican American, Chicano, Latino, Hispanic, Texan, or American.

There is no consensus on how people of Spanish-speaking extraction wish to be known. In *Hispanic Nation* (1996), Geoffrey Fox suggests that whether one is Hispanic may ultimately reside in the individual's own definition of himself:

> The effective definition of Hispanic in contemporary American ethnospeak is

any person who either speaks Spanish as a first language or had some ancestor who did, even if this person only speaks English. Others whose ancestors may never have really mastered Spanish but who had Spanish surnames imposed on them by their conquerors—Mayans, Quechuas, Filipinos, and so on—are often given, and sometimes willingly assume, the label "Hispanic."'

These diverse people are a community only to the extent and only in the ways that they imagine themselves to be. And the only sort of community they can imagine themselves to be is that vague sort we call a "people" or "nation."

This concept of a nation defined by heritage, not geography, is perhaps the most significant distinction between Americans whom we broadly define as Native American and those whom we call Hispanic. Though Fox observes that "Spanish speakers and their descendants from places as widely separated as Chile and Mexico often feel *simpatía*, a recognition of themselves in the other, that they do not have with non-Hispanics," the concept of a cohesive Hispanic nation is not commonly held. Nor do Hispanics have a common history, except those in the United States who view October 12, 1492, the date of Columbus's discovery of the New World, as *El Día de la Raza*, "The Day of the Race."

But Hispanics do share one unifying trait: a common language, which functions as a "mark of membership" and a "source of pride," according to Fox. The Spanish language connects U.S. Hispanics to a noble literary tradition that includes Miguel de Cervantes and Pedro Calderón de la Barca, Federico García Lorca and Rubén Darío, Pablo Neruda, Octavio Paz, Jorge Luis Borges, and Gabriel García Márquez. It also proves invaluable in establishing institutions geared toward serving Spanish-speaking clientele and provides a link among Hispanics in media, advertising, and politics. A common language among such diverse groups as Mexicans, Puerto Ricans, and Cubans not only allows Hispanic Americans to preserve their traditions and identity, but also is an essential way to establish solidarity.

By contrast, Native Americans have spoken hundreds of different languages, some of which, like the natives themselves, have become extinct. The tribal unit as a "nation" can vary from thousands of loosely affiliated members to distinct groups united by biology and history. Though Native American peoples of the 20th century have more or less adapted to the generalized term "Native Americans" in defining their heritage, tribal membership remains the essential criterion for determining who is Indian, both among Native Americans themselves and in their relationships with other Americans.

Five hundred years after Christopher Columbus, it is nearly impossible to answer the question: Who is an Indian? Or: Who is a Hispanic? The degree of intermingling among Native American tribes, Native Americans and Spanish-speaking Americans, and Native Amer-

icans and others of European or African extraction has resulted in intricate blendings of cultures, traditions, biological and physical traits, and identities.

Perhaps the single greatest issue facing both Native Americans and Hispanic Americans is finding the right balance between preserving their unique identity, which many see as separate from mainstream America, and participating as equals in the affairs of the modern world. Like every ethnic group that has immigrated to the United States, Native Americans and Hispanics are torn between preserving their traditional culture and becoming assimilated into the larger culture. Not all individuals or communities choose to resolve that conflict in the same way.

In his 1978 study on the urbanization of American Indians, the anthropologist Sol Tax observed that this balance is crucial to the survival of Native Americans. And as they have survived 500 years of upheaval after the arrival of whites, they will adapt in the modern world as well:

> The lesson is an old one. There are no "Indians," but rather different communities of Indians. . . . Indian people from time immemorial have explored and found ways to live in new environments without losing their identities or values. They "accepted the horse" fully, but nobody supposes they should have become horses. They are . . . fully capable of learning to live with us without becoming like us.

BIBLIOGRAPHY

Bakeless, John. *America as Seen by Its First Explorers: The Eyes of Discovery.* Mineola, NY: Dover Publications, Inc., 1989.

Bee, Robert L. *The Yuma.* New York: Chelsea House Publishers, 1989.

Berdan, Frances F. *The Aztecs.* New York: Chelsea House Publishers, 1989.

Bonvillain, Nancy. *The Zuni.* New York: Chelsea House Publishers, 1995.

Catton, Bruce, and William B. Catton. *The Bold and Magnificent Dream: America's Founding Years 1492–1815.* Garden City, NY: Doubleday & Company, 1978.

Dodge, Stephen C. *Christopher Columbus and the First Voyages to the New World.* New York: Chelsea House Publishers, 1991.

Dolan, Sean. *Juan Ponce de León.* New York: Chelsea House Publishers, 1995.

Dolan, Sean. *Junípero Serra.* New York: Chelsea House Publishers, 1991.

Force, Roland W., and Maryanne Tefft Force. *The American Indians.* New York: Chelsea House Publishers, 1996.

Fox, Geoffrey. *Hispanic Nation: Culture, Politics, and the Constructing of Identity.* Secaucus, NJ: Birch Lane Press, 1996.

Frank, Andrew. *The Birth of Black America: The Age of Discovery and the Slave Trade.* New York: Chelsea House Publishers, 1996.

Garbarino, Merwyn S. *The Seminole.* New York: Chelsea House Publishers, 1989.

Gibson, Robert O. *The Chumash.* New York: Chelsea House Publishers, 1991.

Goetzmann, William H. *New Lands, New Men: America and the Second Great Age of Discovery.* New York: Viking Penguin, Inc., 1986.

Meinig, D. W. *The Shaping of America: A Geographical Perspective on 500 Years of History*. Vol. 1, *Atlantic America, 1492–1800*. New Haven, CT: Yale University Press, 1986.

Morison, Samuel Eliot, Henry Steele Commager, and William E. Leuchtenburg. *The Growth of the American Republic*. Vol. 1. New York: Oxford University Press, 1980.

Morris, John Miller. *From Coronado to Escalante: The Explorers of the Spanish Southwest*. New York: Chelsea House Publishers, 1992.

Ortiz, Alfonso. *The Pueblo*. New York: Chelsea House Publishers, 1994.

Snow, Dean R. *The Archaeology of North America*. New York: Chelsea House Publishers, 1989.

Stannard, David E. *American Holocaust: The Conquest of the New World*. New York: Oxford University Press, 1992.

Steele, Ian K. *Warpaths: Invasions of North America*. New York: Oxford University Press, 1994.

Thornton, Russell. *American Indian Holocaust and Survival: A Population History Since 1492*. Norman: University of Oklahoma Press, 1987.

Waldman, Carl. *Encyclopedia of Native American Tribes*. New York: Facts on File Publications, 1988.

Wepman, Dennis. *Hernán Cortés*. New York: Chelsea House Publishers, 1986.

Whitman, Sylvia. *Hernando de Soto and the Explorers of the American South*. New York: Chelsea House Publishers, 1991.

Winn, Peter. *Americas: The Changing Face of Latin America and the Caribbean*. New York: Pantheon Books, 1992.

GLOSSARY

anthropology the study of the physical, social, and cultural characteristics of human beings. Subdisciplines include archaeology, ethnology, biological anthropology, and linguistics.

Arawak the European name for the Taino (from the native word for "good" or "noble"), who lived in the West Indies at the time of Columbus's arrival.

assimilation the complete absorption of one group into another group's cultural tradition.

atlatl Aztec word for spear-thrower; an implement used to extend the length of a hunter's throwing arm and thereby add force and distance to the throw. Spear-throwers were in general use in North America until they were largely replaced by the bow and arrow around 2,000 years ago.

Black Drink an herbal drink used by south-eastern tribes to induce vomiting as part of a purification ritual.

booger mask a face covering carved to represent evil spirits, worn during the booger dance to express hostility for one's enemies.

burial mound a large earthen construction built by prehistoric American Indians to enclose human graves.

cacique, cacica a Native American village official in areas dominated primarily by Spanish culture.

city-state an autonomous political unit consisting of one major urban center and the smaller communities in the surrounding area.

conquistador Spanish for "conqueror"; a leader in the Spanish conquest of America, Mexico, and Peru in the 16th century.

cosmology the worldview of a specific people encompassing the relationship between humans, supernatural beings, and the natural world.

criollo a person of pure Spanish descent born in Spanish America; a person born and raised in a Latin American country.

culture area a region in which people share cultural traits of a common background or environment, such as language and religious beliefs, and organize into similar economic, social, and political groups.

encomienda a Spanish colonial institution that granted Spanish overlords *(encomenderos)* the privilege of collecting tribute and requiring labor from natives. Encomenderos were responsible for converting their native laborers to Christianity.

entrada Spanish for "entrance"; a Spanish expedition of exploration and conquest in the Americas.

Formative period the period from 1000 B.C. to A.D. 1000, during which agriculture developed and people began settling in permanent communities and trading products and goods with similarly established groups.

Ice Age the period beginning around 1.6 million years ago and ending around 10,000 years ago, during which nearly half of North America was covered by glaciers. Also known as the Pleistocene epoch.

Green Corn Ceremony a southeastern tribal celebration of purification, forgiveness, and thanksgiving held annually when the new crop of corn ripens.

hidalgo a member of the lower nobility of Spain.

hunting and gathering an economic system based on the collection of food by hunting wild animals, fishing, and gathering wild plant foods; the most ancient of human ways of obtaining the necessities of life.

Indian Removal Act the 1830 federal law that authorized the relocation of eastern Indian tribes to lands west of the Mississippi River.

Indian Territory an area in the south central United States to which the U.S. government resettled Indians from other regions, especially the eastern states. In 1907, this area and Oklahoma Territory became the state of Oklahoma.

intermarriage marriage between members of different ethnic or cultural groups.

mesa a flat-topped, tablelike hill.

mestizo a person of mixed Indian-Spanish ancestry who follows Hispanic cultural practices.

miscegenation marriage between members of different races.

mulatto a person of mixed black and white ancestry.

municipality a self-governing political unit; the way in which Spanish towns were organized during North American colonization.

mythology a body of myths or tales dealing with the gods and legendary heroes of a particular people.

nomad (nomadic) a person having no permanent home, who continually moves to find sources of food.

Paleo-Indian period the period in North America lasting until about 10,000 years ago, when human lifeways involved hunting large mammals and making specialized stone tools.

Paleolithic the Old Stone Age of the Eastern Hemisphere, during which human beings evolved to their modern form and which lasted until about 10,000 years ago, out of which came the earliest tool industries of Paleo-Indians.

petroglyph a carving in stone.

pictograph a drawing on stone.

projectile points stone weapon tips that were attached to wooden shafts to form spears, lances, and arrows.

pueblo a southwestern Native American village composed of a complex of several flat-roofed communal homes made of stone or adobe.

Reconquista the Christian military crusade that drove the ruling Moors from Spain in 1492 .

removal policy the national policy of 1830 calling for the sale of all Indian land in the states and the migration of Indians from eastern and southern states to and resettlement in a segregated, exclusively Indian territory (Kansas and Oklahoma). Those Indians who remained in the East came under state laws.

Santa Fe Trail the pioneer commercial route to the Southwest from present-day Kansas City, Missouri, ending in Santa Fe, New Mexico.

shaman a person who has special powers to call on various spirits to solve problems, heal the sick, or ensure success in acquiring food or in other essential activities.

solidarity unity within a group or class that produces or is based upon common interests, objectives, and standards.

Trail of Tears the harsh journey of Cherokee forced out of their homeland in the Southeast by the federal government to their relocation site in what is now Oklahoma; part of a much larger movement of southeastern Native Americans such as the Creek, Chickasaw, Seminole, and Choctaw, who were forced from their homes between 1830 and 1840.

treaty a contract negotiated between representatives of the U.S. government and another sovereign nation, or nations, including Indian tribes. Treaties deal with the cessation of military action, the surrender of political independence, the establishment of boundaries, terms of land sales, and related matters.

tribe a type of society consisting of several or many separate communities united by kinship and such social units as clans, religious organizations, economic and political institutions, a common culture, and language. Tribes are generally characterized by economic and political equality and thus do not have social classes.

INDEX

PICTURE CREDITS

Every effort has been made to contact the copyright owners of photographs and illustrations used in this book. In the event that the holder of a copyright has not heard from us, he or she should contact Chelsea House Publishers.

THERESE DE ANGELIS holds an M.A. in English Literature from Villanova University and studied rare book cataloging and preservation at Columbia University. She was a contributing editor for Chelsea House's *The Black Muslims* and the WOMEN WRITERS OF ENGLISH series. This is her first book for Chelsea House.

FRANK W. PORTER III, general editor of INDIANS OF NORTH AMERICA, is director of the Chelsea House Foundation for American Indian Studies. He holds a B.A., M.A., and Ph.D. from the University of Maryland. He has done extensive research concerning the Indians of Maryland and Delaware and is the author of numerous articles on their history, archaeology, geography, and ethnography. He was formerly director of the Maryland Commission on Indian Affairs and American Indian Research and Resource Institute, Gettysburg, Pennsylvania, and he has received grants from the Delaware Humanities Forum, the Maryland Committee for the Humanities, the Ford Foundation, and the National Endowment for the Humanities, among others. Dr. Porter is the author of *The Bureau of Indian Affairs* in the Chelsea House KNOW YOUR GOVERNMENT series.